THE PAPERS AND WRITINGS OF ABRAHAM LINCOLN

VOLUME ONE
1832-1843

**Special Constitutional Collectors' Edition
Includes The Gettysburg Address and the
Emancipation Proclamation**

Edited by Rutger M. Lamont

With an Introduction by Theodore Roosevelt

The Essay on Lincoln by Carl Schurz

The Address on Lincoln by Joseph Choate

NMD Books
Simi Valley, CA

Copyright 2011 –Abraham Lincoln

Visit our Web site at http://www.NMDbooks.com.

Library of Congress Cataloging-in-Publication Data
THE PAPERS AND WRITINGS OF ABRAHAM LINCOLN
1832-1843
VOLUME ONE - CONSTITUTIONAL EDITION
Includes bibliographical references and index.
ISBN: 978-1-936828-04-3 (Softcover)

First Edition January 2011

Contents

VOLUME 1.

INTRODUCTORY

Immediately after Lincoln's re-election to the Presidency, in an off-hand speech, delivered in response to a serenade by some of his admirers on the evening of November 10, 1864, he spoke as follows:

"It has long been a grave question whether any government not too strong for the liberties of its people can be strong enough to maintain its existence in great emergencies. On this point, the present rebellion brought our republic to a severe test, and the Presidential election, occurring in regular course during the rebellion, added not a little to the strain.... The strife of the election is but human nature practically applied to the facts in the case. What has occurred in this case must ever occur in similar cases. Human nature will not change. In any future great national trial, compared with the men of this, we shall have as weak and as strong, as silly and as wise, as bad and as good. Let us therefore study the incidents in this as philosophy to learn wisdom from and none of them as wrongs to be avenged.... Now that the election is over, may not all having a common interest reunite in a common fort to save our common country? For my own part, I have striven and shall strive to avoid placing any obstacle in the way. So long as I have been here, I have not willingly planted a thorn in any man's bosom. While I am deeply sensible to the high compliment of a re-election and duly grateful, as I trust, to Almighty God for having directed my countrymen to a right conclusion, as I think for their own good, it adds nothing to my satisfaction that any other man may be disappointed or pained by the result."

This speech has not attracted much general attention, yet it is in a peculiar degree both illustrative and typical of the great statesman who made it, alike in its strong common-sense and in its lofty standard of morality. Lincoln's life, Lincoln's deeds and words, are not only of consuming interest to the historian, but should be intimately known to every man engaged in the hard practical work of American political life. It is difficult to overstate how much it means to a nation to have as the two foremost figures in its history men like Washington and Lincoln. It is good for every man in any way concerned in public life to feel that the highest ambition any American can possibly have will be gratified just in proportion as he raises himself toward the standards set by these two men.

It is a very poor thing, whether for nations or individuals, to advance the history of great deeds done in the past as an excuse for doing poorly in the present; but it is an excellent thing to study the history of the great deeds of the past, and of the great men who did them, with an earnest desire to profit thereby so as to render better service in the present. In their essentials, the men of the present day are much like the men of the past, and the live issues of the present can be faced to better advantage by men who have in good faith studied how the leaders of the nation faced the dead issues of the past. Such a study of Lincoln's life will enable us to avoid the twin gulfs of immorality and inefficiency—the gulfs which always lie one on each side of the careers alike of man and of nation. It helps nothing to have avoided one if shipwreck is encountered in the other. The fanatic, the well-meaning moralist of unbalanced mind, the parlor critic who condemns others but has no power himself to do good and but little power to do ill—all these were as alien to Lincoln as the vicious and unpatriotic themselves. His life teaches our people that they must act with wisdom, because otherwise adherence to right will be mere sound and fury without substance; and that they must also act high-mindedly, or else what seems to be wisdom will in the end turn out to be the most destructive kind of folly.

Throughout his entire life, and especially after he rose to leadership in his party, Lincoln was stirred to his depths by the sense of fealty to a lofty ideal; but throughout his entire life, he also accepted human nature as it is, and worked with keen, practical good sense to achieve results with the instruments at hand. It is impossible to conceive of a man farther removed from baseness, farther removed from corruption, from mere self-seeking; but it is also impossible to conceive of a man of more sane and healthy mind—a man less under the influence of that fantastic and diseased morality (so fantastic and diseased as to be in reality profoundly immoral) which makes a man in this work-a-day world refuse to do what is possible because he cannot accomplish the impossible.

In the fifth volume of Lecky's History of England, the historian draws an interesting distinction between the qualities needed for a successful political career in modern society and those which lead to eminence in the spheres of pure intellect or pure moral effort. He says:

"....the moral qualities that are required in the higher spheres of statesmanship [are not] those of a hero or a saint. Passionate earnestness and self-devotion, complete concentration of every faculty on an unselfish aim, uncalculating daring, a delicacy of conscience and a loftiness of aim far exceeding those of the average of men, are here likely to prove rather a hindrance than an assistance. The politician deals very largely with the superficial and the commonplace; his art is in a great measure that of skilful compromise, and in the conditions of modern life, the statesman is likely to succeed best who possesses secondary qualities to an unusual degree, who is in the closest intellectual and moral sympathy with the average of the intelligent men of his time, and who pursues common ideals with more than common ability.... Tact, business talent, knowledge of men, resolution, promptitude and sagacity in dealing with immediate emergencies, a character which lends itself easily to conciliation, diminishes friction and inspires confidence, are especially needed, and they are more likely to be found among shrewd and enlightened men of the world than among men of great original genius or of an heroic type of character."

The American people should feel profoundly grateful that the greatest American statesman since Washington, the statesman who in this absolutely democratic republic succeeded best, was the very man who actually combined the two sets of qualities which the historian thus puts in antithesis. Abraham Lincoln, the rail-splitter, the Western country lawyer, was one of the shrewdest and most enlightened men of the world, and he had all the practical qualities which enable such a man to guide his countrymen; and yet he was also a genius of the heroic type, a leader who rose level to the greatest crisis through which this nation or any other nation had to pass in the nineteenth century.

THEODORE ROOSEVELT
SAGAMORE HILL, OYSTER BAY, N. Y., September 22, 1905.

INTRODUCTORY NOTE

"I have endured," wrote Lincoln not long before his death, "a great deal of ridicule without much malice, and have received a great deal of kindness not quite free from ridicule." On Easter Day, 1865, the world knew how little this ridicule, how much this kindness, had really signified. Thereafter, Lincoln the man became Lincoln the hero, year by year more heroic, until to-day, with the swift passing of those who knew him, his figure grows ever dimmer, less real. This should not be. For Lincoln the man, patient, wise, set in a high resolve, is worth far more than Lincoln the hero, vaguely glorious. Invaluable is the example of the man, intangible that of the hero.

And, though it is not for us, as for those who in awed stillness listened at Gettysburg with inspired perception, to know Abraham Lincoln, yet there is for us another way whereby we may attain such knowledge—through his words—uttered in all sincerity to those who loved or hated him. Cold, unsatisfying they may seem, these printed words, while we can yet speak with those who knew him, and look into eyes that once looked into his. But in truth it is here that we find his simple greatness, his great simplicity, and though no man tried less so to show his power, no man has so shown it more clearly.

Thus these writings of Abraham Lincoln are associated with those of Washington, Hamilton, Franklin, and of the other "Founders of the Republic," not that Lincoln should become still more of the past, but, rather, that he with them should become still more of the present. However faint and mythical may grow the story of that Great Struggle, the leader, Lincoln, at least should remain a real, living American. No matter how clearly, how directly, Lincoln has shown himself in his writings, we yet should not forget those men whose minds, from their various view-points, have illumined for us his character. As this nation owes a great debt to Lincoln, so, also, Lincoln's memory owes a great debt to a nation which, as no other nation could have done, has been able to appreciate his full worth. Among the many who have brought about this appreciation, those only whose estimates have been placed in these volumes may be mentioned here. To President Roosevelt, to Mr. Schurz and to Mr. Choate, the editor, for himself, for the publishers, and on behalf of the readers, wishes to offer his sincere acknowledgments.

Thanks are also due, for valuable and sympathetic assistance rendered in the preparation of this work, to Mr. Gilbert A. Tracy, of

Putnam, Conn., Major William H. Lambert, of Philadelphia, and Mr. C. F. Gunther, of Chicago, to the Chicago Historical Association and personally to its capable Secretary, Miss McIlvaine, to Major Henry S. Burrage, of Portland, Me., and to General Thomas J. Henderson, of Illinois.

For various courtesies received, the editor is furthermore indebted to the Librarian of the Library of Congress; to Messrs. McClure, Phillips & Co., D. Appleton & Co., Macmillan & Co., Dodd, Mead & Co., and Harper Brothers, of New York; to Houghton, Mifflin & Co., Dana, Estes & Co., and L. C. Page & Co., of Boston; to A. C. McClure & Co., of Chicago; to The Robert Clarke Co., of Cincinnati, and to the J. B. Lippincott Co., of Philadelphia.

It is hardly necessary to add that every effort has been made by the editor to bring into these volumes whatever material may there properly belong, material much of which is widely scattered in public libraries and in private collections. He has been fortunate in securing certain interesting correspondence and papers which had not before come into print in book form. Information concerning some of these papers had reached him too late to enable the papers to find place in their proper chronological order in the set. Rather, however, than not to present these papers to the readers they have been included in the seventh volume of the set, which concludes the "Writings."

October, 1905, A. B. L.

ABRAHAM LINCOLN: AN ESSAY BY CARL SHURZ

No American can study the character and career of Abraham Lincoln without being carried away by sentimental emotions. We are always inclined to idealize that which we love,—a state of mind very unfavorable to the exercise of sober critical judgment. It is therefore not surprising that most of those who have written or spoken on that extraordinary man, even while conscientiously endeavoring to draw a lifelike portraiture of his being, and to form a just estimate of his public conduct, should have drifted into more or less indiscriminating eulogy, painting his great features in the most glowing colors, and covering with tender shadings whatever might look like a blemish.

But his standing before posterity will not be exalted by mere praise of his virtues and abilities, nor by any concealment of his limitations and faults. The stature of the great man, one of whose peculiar charms consisted in his being so unlike all other great men, will rather lose than gain by the idealization which so easily runs into the commonplace. For it was distinctly the weird mixture of qualities and forces in him, of the lofty with the common, the ideal with the uncouth, of that which he had become with that which he had not ceased to be, that made him so fascinating a character among his fellow-men, gave him his singular power over their minds and hearts, and fitted him to be the greatest leader in the greatest crisis of our national life.

His was indeed a marvellous growth. The statesman or the military hero born and reared in a log cabin is a familiar figure in American history; but we may search in vain among our celebrities for one whose origin and early life equalled Abraham Lincoln's in wretchedness. He first saw the light in a miserable hovel in Kentucky, on a farm consisting of a few barren acres in a dreary neighborhood; his father a typical "poor Southern white," shiftless and without ambition for himself or his children, constantly looking for a new piece of land on which he might make a living without much work; his mother, in her youth handsome and bright, grown prematurely coarse in feature and soured in mind by daily toil and care; the whole household squalid, cheerless, and utterly void of elevating inspirations... Only when the family had "moved" into the malarious backwoods of Indiana, the mother had died, and a stepmother, a woman of thrift and energy, had taken charge of the children, the shaggy-headed, ragged, barefooted, forlorn boy, then seven years old, "began to feel like a human being." Hard work was his early lot. When a mere boy he had to help in supporting the family, either on his father's clearing, or hired out to other farmers to plough, or dig ditches, or chop wood, or drive ox teams; occasionally also to "tend the baby," when the farmer's wife was otherwise engaged. He could regard it as an advancement to a higher sphere of activity when he obtained work in a "crossroads store," where he amused the customers by his talk over the counter; for he soon distinguished himself among the backwoods folk as one who had something to say worth listening to. To win that distinction, he had to draw mainly upon his wits; for, while his thirst for knowledge was great, his opportunities for satisfying that thirst were wofully slender.

In the log schoolhouse, which he could visit but little, he was taught only reading, writing, and elementary arithmetic. Among the people of the settlement, bush farmers and small tradesmen, he found none of uncommon intelligence or education; but some of them had a few books, which he borrowed eagerly. Thus he read and reread, AEsop's Fables, learning to tell stories with a point and to argue by parables; he read Robinson Crusoe, The Pilgrim's Progress, a short history of the United States, and Weems's Life of Washington. To the town constable's he went to read the Revised Statutes of Indiana. Every printed page that fell into his hands he would greedily devour, and his family and friends watched him with wonder, as the uncouth boy, after his daily work, crouched in a corner of the log cabin or outside under a tree, absorbed in a book while munching his supper of corn bread. In this manner he began to gather some knowledge, and sometimes he would astonish the girls with such startling remarks as that the earth was moving around the sun, and not the sun around the earth, and they marvelled where "Abe" could have got such queer notions. Soon he also felt the impulse to write; not only making extracts from books he wished to remember, but also composing little essays of his own. First he sketched these with charcoal on a wooden shovel scraped white with a drawing-knife, or on basswood shingles. Then he transferred them to paper, which was a scarce commodity in the Lincoln household; taking care to cut his expressions close, so that they might not cover too much space,—a style-forming method greatly to be commended. Seeing boys put a burning coal on the back of a wood turtle, he was moved to write on cruelty to animals. Seeing men intoxicated with whiskey, he wrote on temperance. In verse-making, too, he tried himself, and in satire on persons offensive to him or others,—satire the rustic wit of which was not always fit for ears polite. Also political thoughts he put upon paper, and some of his pieces were even deemed good enough for publication in the county weekly.

Thus he won a neighborhood reputation as a clever young man, which he increased by his performances as a speaker, not seldom drawing upon himself the dissatisfaction of his employers by mounting a stump in the field, and keeping the farm hands from their work by little speeches in a jocose and sometimes also a serious vein. At the rude social frolics of the settlement he became an important person, telling funny, stories, mimicking the itinerant preachers who had happened to pass by, and making his mark at wrestling matches, too; for at the age of seventeen he had attained his full height, six feet four inches in his stockings, if he had any, and a terribly muscular clodhopper he was. But he was known never to use his extraordinary strength to the injury or humiliation of others; rather to do them a kindly turn, or to enforce justice and fair dealing between them. All this made him a favorite in backwoods society, although in some things he appeared a little odd, to his friends. Far more than any of them, he was given not only to reading, but to fits of abstraction, to quiet musing with himself, and also to strange spells of melancholy, from which he often would pass in a moment to rollicking outbursts of droll humor. But on the whole he was one of the people among whom he lived; in appearance perhaps even a little more uncouth than most of them,—a very tall, rawboned youth, with large features, dark, shrivelled skin, and rebellious hair; his arms and legs long, out of proportion; clad in deerskin trousers, which from frequent exposure to the rain had shrunk so as to sit tightly on his limbs, leaving several inches of bluish shin exposed between their lower end and the heavy tan-colored shoes; the nether garment held usually by only one suspender, that was strung over a coarse homemade shirt; the head covered in winter with a coonskin cap, in summer with a rough straw hat of uncertain shape, without a band.

It is doubtful whether he felt himself much superior to his surroundings, although he confessed to a yearning for some knowledge of the world outside of the circle in which he lived. This wish was gratified; but how? At the age of nineteen he went down the Mississippi to New Orleans as a flatboat hand, temporarily joining a trade many members of which at that time still took pride in being

14

called "half horse and half alligator." After his return he worked and lived in the old way until the spring of 1830, when his father "moved again," this time to Illinois; and on the journey of fifteen days "Abe" had to drive the ox wagon which carried the household goods. Another log cabin was built, and then, fencing a field, Abraham Lincoln split those historic rails which were destined to play so picturesque a part in the Presidential campaign twenty-eight years later.

Having come of age, Lincoln left the family, and "struck out for himself." He had to "take jobs whenever he could get them." The first of these carried him again as a flatboat hand to New Orleans. There something happened that made a lasting impression upon his soul: he witnessed a slave auction. "His heart bled," wrote one of his companions; "said nothing much; was silent; looked bad. I can say, knowing it, that it was on this trip that he formed his opinion on slavery. It run its iron in him then and there, May, 1831. I have heard him say so often." Then he lived several years at New Salem, in Illinois, a small mushroom village, with a mill, some "stores" and whiskey shops, that rose quickly, and soon disappeared again. It was a desolate, disjointed, half-working and half-loitering life, without any other aim than to gain food and shelter from day to day. He served as pilot on a steamboat trip, then as clerk in a store and a mill; business failing, he was adrift for some time. Being compelled to measure his strength with the chief bully of the neighborhood, and overcoming him, he became a noted person in that muscular community, and won the esteem and friendship of the ruling gang of ruffians to such a degree that, when the Black Hawk war broke out, they elected him, a young man of twenty-three, captain of a volunteer company, composed mainly of roughs of their kind. He took the field, and his most noteworthy deed of valor consisted, not in killing an Indian, but in protecting against his own men, at the peril of his own life, the life of an old savage who had strayed into his camp.

The Black Hawk war over, he turned to politics. The step from the captaincy of a volunteer company to a candidacy for a seat in the Legislature seemed a natural one. But his popularity, although great in New Salem, had not spread far enough over the district, and he was defeated. Then the wretched hand-to-mouth struggle began again. He "set up in store-business" with a dissolute partner, who drank whiskey while Lincoln was reading books. The result was a disastrous failure and a load of debt. Thereupon he became a deputy surveyor, and was appointed postmaster of New Salem, the business of the post-office being so small that he could carry the incoming and outgoing mail in his hat. All this could not lift him from poverty, and his surveying instruments and horse and saddle were sold by the sheriff for debt.

But while all this misery was upon him his ambition rose to higher aims. He walked many miles to borrow from a schoolmaster a grammar with which to improve his language. A lawyer lent him a copy of Blackstone, and he began to study law.

People would look wonderingly at the grotesque figure lying in the grass, "with his feet up a tree," or sitting on a fence, as, absorbed in a book, he learned to construct correct sentences and made himself a jurist. At once he gained a little practice, pettifogging before a justice of the peace for friends, without expecting a fee. Judicial functions, too, were thrust upon him, but only at horse-races or wrestling matches, where his acknowledged honesty and fairness gave his verdicts undisputed authority. His popularity grew apace, and soon he could be a candidate for the Legislature again. Although he called himself a Whig, an ardent admirer of Henry Clay, his clever stump speeches won him the election in the strongly Democratic district. Then for the first time, perhaps, he thought seriously of his outward appearance. So far he had been content with a garb of "Kentucky jeans," not seldom ragged, usually patched, and always shabby. Now, he borrowed some money from a friend to buy a new suit of clothes—"store clothes" fit for a Sangamon County statesman; and thus adorned he set out for the state capital, Vandalia, to take his seat among the lawmakers.

His legislative career, which stretched over several sessions—for he was thrice re-elected, in 1836, 1838, and 1840—was not remarkably brilliant. He did, indeed, not lack ambition. He dreamed even of making himself "the De Witt Clinton of Illinois," and he actually distinguished himself by zealous and effective work in those "log-rolling" operations by which the young State received "a general system of internal improvements" in the shape of railroads, canals, and banks,—a reckless policy, burdening the State with debt, and producing the usual crop of political demoralization, but a policy characteristic of the time and the impatiently enterprising spirit of the Western people. Lincoln, no doubt with the best intentions, but with little knowledge of the subject, simply followed the popular current. The achievement in which, perhaps, he gloried most was the removal of the State government from Vandalia to Springfield; one of those triumphs of political management which are apt to be the pride of the small politician's statesmanship. One thing, however, he did in which his true nature asserted itself, and which gave distinct promise of the future pursuit of high aims. Against an overwhelming preponderance of sentiment in the Legislature, followed by only one other member, he recorded his protest against a proslavery resolution,—that protest declaring "the institution of slavery to be founded on both injustice and bad policy." This was not only the irrepressible voice of his conscience; it was true moral valor, too; for at that time, in many parts of the West, an abolitionist was regarded as little better than a horse-thief, and even "Abe Lincoln" would hardly have been forgiven his antislavery principles, had he not been known as such an "uncommon good fellow." But here, in obedience to the great conviction of his life, he manifested his courage to stand alone, that courage which is the first requisite of leadership in a great cause.

Together with his reputation and influence as a politician grew his law practice, especially after he had removed from New Salem to Springfield, and associated himself with a practitioner of good standing. He had now at last won a fixed position in society. He became a successful lawyer, less, indeed, by his learning as a jurist than by his effectiveness as an advocate and by the striking uprightness of his character; and it may truly be said that his vivid sense of truth and justice had much to do with his effectiveness as an advocate. He would refuse to act as the attorney even of personal friends when he saw the right on the other side. He would abandon cases, even during trial, when the testimony convinced him that his client was in the wrong. He would dissuade those who sought his service from pursuing an obtainable advantage when their claims seemed to him unfair. Presenting his very first case in the United States Circuit Court, the only question being one of authority, he declared that, upon careful examination, he found all the authorities on the other side, and none on his. Persons accused of crime, when he thought them guilty, he would not defend at all, or, attempting their defence, he was unable to put forth his powers. One notable exception is on record, when his personal sympathies had been strongly aroused. But when he felt himself to be the protector of innocence, the defender of justice, or the prosecutor of wrong, he frequently disclosed such unexpected resources of reasoning, such depth of feeling, and rose to such fervor of appeal as to astonish and overwhelm his hearers, and make him fairly irresistible. Even an ordinary law argument, coming from him, seldom failed to produce the impression that he was profoundly convinced of the soundness of his position. It is not surprising that the mere appearance of so conscientious an attorney in any case should have carried, not only to juries, but even to judges, almost a presumption of right on his side, and that the people began to call him, sincerely meaning it, "honest Abe Lincoln."

In the meantime he had private sorrows and trials of a painfully afflicting nature. He had loved and been loved by a fair and estimable girl, Ann Rutledge, who died in the flower of her youth and beauty, and he mourned her loss with such intensity of grief that his friends feared for his reason. Recovering from his morbid depression, he bestowed what he thought a new affection upon another lady, who refused him. And finally, moderately prosperous in his worldly affairs, and having prospects of political distinction before him, he paid his addresses to Mary Todd, of Kentucky, and was accepted. But then tormenting doubts of the genuineness of his own affection for her, of the compatibility of their characters, and of their future happiness came upon him. His distress was so great that he felt himself in danger of suicide, and feared to carry a pocket-knife with him; and he gave mortal offence to his bride by not appearing on the appointed wedding day. Now the torturing consciousness of the wrong he had done her grew unendurable. He won back her affection, ended the agony by marrying her, and became a faithful and patient husband and a good father. But it was no secret to those who knew the family well that his domestic life was full of trials. The erratic temper of his wife not seldom put the gentleness of his nature to the severest tests; and these troubles and struggles, which accompanied him through all the vicissitudes of his life from the modest home in Springfield to the White House at Washington, adding untold private heart-burnings to his public cares, and sometimes precipitating upon him incredible embarrassments in the discharge of his public duties, form one of the most pathetic features of his career.

He continued to "ride the circuit," read books while travelling in his buggy, told funny stories to his fellow-lawyers in the tavern, chatted familiarly with his neighbors around the stove in the store and at the post-office, had his hours of melancholy brooding as of old, and became more and more widely known and trusted and beloved among the people of his State for his ability as a lawyer and politician, for the uprightness of his character and the overflowing spring of sympathetic kindness in his heart. His main ambition was confessedly that of political distinction; but hardly any one would at that time have seen in him the man destined to lead the nation through the greatest crisis of the century.

His time had not yet come when, in 1846, he was elected to Congress. In a clever speech in the House of Representatives he denounced President Polk for having unjustly forced war upon Mexico, and he amused the Committee of the Whole by a witty attack upon General Cass. More important was the expression he gave to his antislavery impulses by offering a bill looking to the emancipation of the slaves in the District of Columbia, and by his repeated votes for the famous Wilmot Proviso, intended to exclude slavery from the Territories acquired from Mexico. But when, at the expiration of his term, in March, 1849, he left his seat, he gloomily despaired of ever seeing the day when the cause nearest to his heart would be rightly grasped by the people, and when he would be able to render any service to his country in solving the great problem. Nor had his career as a member of Congress in any sense been such as to gratify his ambition. Indeed, if he ever had any belief in a great destiny for himself, it must have been weak at that period; for he actually sought to obtain from the new Whig President, General Taylor, the place of Commissioner of the General Land Office; willing to bury himself in one of the administrative bureaus of the government. Fortunately for the country, he failed; and no less fortunately, when, later, the territorial governorship of Oregon was offered to him, Mrs. Lincoln's protest induced him to decline it. Returning to Springfield, he gave himself with renewed zest to his law practice, acquiesced in the Compromise of 1850 with reluctance and a mental reservation, supported in the Presidential campaign of 1852 the Whig candidate in some spiritless speeches, and took but a languid interest in the politics of the day. But just then his time was drawing near.

The peace promised, and apparently inaugurated, by the Compromise of 1850 was rudely broken by the introduction of the Kansas-Nebraska Bill in 1854. The repeal of the Missouri Compromise, opening the Territories of the United States, the heritage of coming generations, to the invasion of slavery, suddenly revealed the whole significance of the slavery question to the people of the free States, and thrust itself into the politics of the country as the paramount issue. Something like an electric shock flashed through the North. Men who but a short time before had been absorbed by their business pursuits, and deprecated all political agitation, were startled out of their security by a sudden alarm, and excitedly took sides. That restless trouble of conscience about slavery, which even in times of apparent repose had secretly disturbed the souls of Northern people, broke forth in an utterance louder than ever. The bonds of accustomed party allegiance gave way. Antislavery Democrats and antislavery Whigs felt themselves drawn together by a common overpowering sentiment, and soon they began to rally in a new organization. The Republican party sprang into being to meet the overruling call of the hour. Then Abraham Lincoln's time was come. He rapidly advanced to a position of conspicuous championship in the struggle. This, however, was not owing to his virtues and abilities alone. Indeed, the slavery question stirred his soul in its profoundest depths; it was, as one of his intimate friends said, "the only one on which he would become excited"; it called forth all his faculties and energies. Yet there were many others who, having long and arduously fought the antislavery battle in the popular assembly, or in the press, or in the halls of Congress, far surpassed him in prestige, and compared with whom he was still an obscure and untried man. His reputation, although highly honorable and well earned, had so far been essentially local. As a stump-speaker in Whig canvasses outside of his State he had attracted comparatively little attention; but in Illinois he had been recognized as one of the foremost men of the Whig party. Among the opponents of the Nebraska Bill he occupied in his State so important a position, that in 1856 he was the choice of a large majority of the "Anti-Nebraska men" in the Legislature for a seat in the Senate of the United States which then became vacant; and when he, an old Whig, could not obtain the votes of the Anti-Nebraska Democrats necessary to make a majority, he generously urged his friends to transfer their votes to Lyman Trumbull, who was then elected. Two years later, in the first national convention of the Republican party, the delegation from Illinois brought him forward as a candidate for the vice-presidency, and he received respectable support. Still, the name of Abraham Lincoln was not widely known beyond the boundaries of his own State. But now it was this local prominence in Illinois that put him in a position of peculiar advantage on the battlefield of national politics. In the assault on the Missouri Compromise which broke down all legal barriers to the spread of slavery Stephen Arnold Douglas was the ostensible leader and central figure; and Douglas was a Senator from Illinois, Lincoln's State. Douglas's national theatre of action was the Senate, but in his constituency in Illinois were the roots of his official position and power. What he did in the Senate he had to justify before the people of Illinois, in order to maintain himself in place; and in Illinois all eyes turned to Lincoln as Douglas's natural antagonist.

As very young men they had come to Illinois, Lincoln from Indiana, Douglas from Vermont, and had grown up together in public life, Douglas as a Democrat, Lincoln as a Whig. They had met first in Vandalia, in 1834, when Lincoln was in the Legislature and Douglas in the lobby; and again in 1836, both as members of the Legislature. Douglas, a very able politician, of the agile, combative, audacious, "pushing" sort, rose in political distinction with remarkable rapidity. In quick succession he became a member of the Legislature, a State's attorney, secretary of state, a judge on the supreme bench of Illinois, three times a Representative in Congress, and a Senator of the United States when only thirty-nine years old. In the National Democratic convention of 1852 he appeared even as an aspirant to the nomination for the Presidency, as the favorite of "young America," and received a respectable vote. He had far outstripped Lincoln in what is commonly called political success and in reputation. But it had frequently happened that in political campaigns Lincoln felt himself impelled, or was selected by his Whig friends, to answer Douglas's speeches; and thus the two were looked upon, in a large part of the State at least, as the representative combatants of their respective parties in the debates before popular meetings. As soon, therefore, as, after the passage of his Kansas-Nebraska Bill, Douglas returned to Illinois to defend his cause before his constituents, Lincoln, obeying not only his own impulse, but also general expectation, stepped forward as his principal opponent. Thus the struggle about the principles involved in the Kansas-Nebraska Bill, or, in a broader sense, the struggle between freedom and slavery, assumed in Illinois the outward form of a personal contest between Lincoln and Douglas; and, as it continued and became more animated, that personal contest in Illinois was watched with constantly increasing interest by the whole country. When, in 1858, Douglas's senatorial term being about to expire, Lincoln was formally designated by the Republican convention of Illinois as their candidate for the Senate, to take Douglas's place, and the two contestants agreed to debate the questions at issue face to face in a series of public meetings, the eyes of the whole American people were turned eagerly to that one point: and the spectacle reminded one of those lays of ancient times telling of two armies, in battle array, standing still to see their two principal champions fight out the contested cause between the lines in single combat.

Lincoln had then reached the full maturity of his powers. His equipment as a statesman did not embrace a comprehensive knowledge of public affairs. What he had studied he had indeed made his own, with the eager craving and that zealous tenacity characteristic of superior minds learning under difficulties. But his narrow opportunities and the unsteady life he had led during his younger years had not permitted the accumulation of large stores in his mind. It is true, in political campaigns he had occasionally spoken on the ostensible issues between the Whigs and the Democrats, the tariff, internal improvements, banks, and so on, but only in a perfunctory manner. Had he ever given much serious thought and study to these subjects, it is safe to assume that a mind so prolific of original conceits as his would certainly have produced some utterance upon them worth remembering. His soul had evidently never been deeply stirred by such topics. But when his moral nature was aroused, his brain developed an untiring activity until it had mastered all the knowledge within reach. As soon as the repeal of the Missouri Compromise had thrust the slavery question into politics as the paramount issue, Lincoln plunged into an arduous study of all its legal, historical, and moral aspects, and then his mind became a complete arsenal of argument. His rich natural gifts, trained by long and varied practice, had made him an orator of rare persuasiveness. In his immature days, he had pleased himself for a short period with that inflated, high-flown style which, among the uncultivated, passes for "beautiful speaking." His inborn truthfulness and his artistic instinct soon overcame that aberration and revealed to him the noble beauty and strength of simplicity. He possessed an uncommon power of clear and compact statement, which might have reminded those who knew the story of his early youth of the efforts of the poor boy, when he copied his compositions from the scraped wooden shovel, carefully to trim his expressions in order to save paper. His language had the energy of honest directness and he was a master of logical lucidity. He loved to point and enliven his reasoning by humorous illustrations, usually anecdotes of Western life, of which he had an inexhaustible store at his command. These anecdotes had not seldom a flavor of rustic robustness about them, but he used them with great effect, while amusing the audience, to give life to an abstraction, to explode an absurdity, to clinch an argument, to drive home an admonition. The natural kindliness of his tone, softening prejudice and disarming partisan rancor, would often open to his reasoning a way into minds most unwilling to receive it.

Yet his greatest power consisted in the charm of his individuality. That charm did not, in the ordinary way, appeal to the ear or to the eye. His voice was not melodious; rather shrill and piercing, especially when it rose to its high treble in moments of great animation. His figure was unhandsome, and the action of his unwieldy limbs awkward. He commanded none of the outward graces of oratory as they are commonly understood. His charm was of a different kind. It flowed from the rare depth and genuineness of his convictions and his sympathetic feelings. Sympathy was the strongest element in his nature. One of his biographers, who knew him before he became President, says: "Lincoln's compassion might be stirred deeply by an object present, but never by an object absent and unseen. In the former case he would most likely extend relief, with little inquiry into the merits of the case, because, as he expressed it himself, it 'took a pain out of his own heart.'" Only half of this is correct. It is certainly true that he could not witness any individual distress or oppression, or any kind of suffering, without feeling a pang of pain himself, and that by relieving as much as he could the suffering of others he put an end to his own. This compassionate impulse to help he felt not only for human beings, but for every living creature. As in his boyhood he angrily reproved the boys who tormented a wood turtle by putting a burning coal on its back, so, we are told, he would, when a mature man, on a journey, dismount from his buggy and wade waist-deep in mire to rescue a pig struggling in a swamp. Indeed, appeals to his compassion were so irresistible to him, and he felt it so difficult to refuse anything when his refusal could give pain, that he himself sometimes spoke of his inability to say "no" as a positive weakness. But that certainly does not prove that his compassionate feeling was confined to individual cases of suffering witnessed with his own eyes. As the boy was moved by the aspect of the tortured wood turtle to compose an essay against cruelty to animals in general, so the aspect of other cases of suffering and wrong wrought up his moral nature, and set his mind to work against cruelty, injustice, and oppression in general.

As his sympathy went forth to others, it attracted others to him. Especially those whom he called the "plain people" felt themselves drawn to him by the instinctive feeling that he understood, esteemed, and appreciated them. He had grown up among the poor, the lowly, the ignorant. He never ceased to remember the good souls he had met among them, and the many kindnesses they had done him. Although in his mental development he had risen far above them, he never looked down upon them. How they felt and how they reasoned he knew, for so he had once felt and reasoned himself. How they could be moved he knew, for so he had once been moved himself and practised moving others. His mind was much larger than theirs, but it thoroughly comprehended theirs; and while he thought much farther than they, their thoughts were ever present to him. Nor had the visible distance between them grown as wide as his rise in the world would seem to have warranted. Much of his backwoods speech and manners still clung to him. Although he had become "Mr. Lincoln" to his later acquaintances, he was still "Abe" to the "Nats" and "Billys" and "Daves" of his youth; and their familiarity neither appeared unnatural to them, nor was it in the least awkward to him. He still told and enjoyed stories similar to those he had told and enjoyed in the Indiana settlement and at New Salem. His wants remained as modest as they had ever been; his domestic habits had by no means completely accommodated themselves to those of his more highborn wife; and though the "Kentucky jeans" apparel had long been dropped, his clothes of better material and better make would sit ill sorted on his gigantic limbs. His cotton umbrella, without a handle, and tied together with a coarse string to keep it from flapping, which he carried on his circuit rides, is said to be remembered still by some of his surviving neighbors. This rusticity of habit was utterly free from that affected contempt of refinement and comfort which self-made men sometimes carry into their more affluent circumstances. To Abraham Lincoln it was entirely natural, and all those who came into contact with him knew it to be so. In his ways of thinking and feeling he had become a gentleman in the highest sense, but the refining process had polished but little the outward form. The plain people, therefore, still considered "honest Abe Lincoln" one of themselves; and when they felt, which they no doubt frequently did, that his thoughts and aspirations moved in a sphere above their own, they were all the more proud of him, without any diminution of fellow-feeling. It was this relation of mutual sympathy and understanding between Lincoln and the plain people that gave him his peculiar power as a public man, and singularly fitted him, as we shall see, for that leadership which was preeminently required in the great crisis then coming on,—the leadership which indeed thinks and moves ahead of the masses, but always remains within sight and sympathetic touch of them.

He entered upon the campaign of 1858 better equipped than he had ever been before. He not only instinctively felt, but he had convinced himself by arduous study, that in this struggle against the spread of slavery he had right, justice, philosophy, the enlightened opinion of mankind, history, the Constitution, and good policy on his side. It was observed that after he began to discuss the slavery question his speeches were pitched in a much loftier key than his former oratorical efforts. While he remained fond of telling funny stories in private conversation, they disappeared more and more from his public discourse. He would still now and then point his argument with expressions of inimitable quaintness, and flash out rays of kindly humor and witty irony; but his general tone was serious, and rose sometimes to genuine solemnity. His masterly skill in dialectical thrust and parry, his wealth of knowledge, his power of reasoning and elevation of sentiment, disclosed in language of rare precision, strength, and beauty, not seldom astonished his old friends.

Neither of the two champions could have found a more formidable antagonist than each now met in the other. Douglas was by far the most conspicuous member of his party. His admirers had dubbed him "the Little Giant," contrasting in that nickname the greatness of his mind with the smallness of his body. But though of low stature, his broad-shouldered figure appeared uncommonly sturdy, and there was something lion-like in the squareness of his brow and jaw, and in the defiant shake of his long hair. His loud and persistent advocacy of territorial expansion, in the name of patriotism and "manifest destiny," had given him an enthusiastic following among the young and ardent. Great natural parts, a highly combative temperament, and long training had made him a debater unsurpassed in a Senate filled with able men. He could be as forceful in his appeals to patriotic feelings as he was fierce in denunciation and thoroughly skilled in all the baser tricks of parliamentary pugilism. While genial and rollicking in his social intercourse—the idol of the "boys" he felt himself one of the most renowned statesmen of his time, and would frequently meet his opponents with an overbearing haughtiness, as persons more to be pitied than to be feared. In his speech opening the campaign of 1858, he spoke of Lincoln, whom the Republicans had dared to advance as their candidate for "his" place in the Senate, with an air of patronizing if not contemptuous condescension, as "a kind, amiable, and intelligent gentleman and a good citizen." The Little Giant would have been pleased to pass off his antagonist as a tall dwarf. He knew Lincoln too well, however, to indulge himself seriously in such a delusion. But the political situation was at that moment in a curious tangle, and Douglas could expect to derive from the confusion great advantage over his opponent.

By the repeal of the Missouri Compromise, opening the Territories to the ingress of slavery, Douglas had pleased the South, but greatly alarmed the North. He had sought to conciliate Northern sentiment by appending to his Kansas-Nebraska Bill the declaration that its intent was "not to legislate slavery into any State or Territory, nor to exclude it therefrom, but to leave the people thereof perfectly free to form and regulate their institutions in their own way, subject only to the Constitution of the United States." This he called "the great principle of popular sovereignty." When asked whether, under this act, the people of a Territory, before its admission as a State, would have the right to exclude slavery, he answered, "That is a question for the courts to decide." Then came the famous "Dred Scott decision," in which the Supreme Court held substantially that the right to hold slaves as property existed in the Territories by virtue of the Federal Constitution, and that this right could not be denied by any act of a territorial government. This, of course, denied the right of the people of any Territory to exclude slavery while they were in a territorial condition, and it alarmed the Northern people still more. Douglas recognized the binding force of the decision of the Supreme Court, at the same time maintaining, most illogically, that his great principle of popular sovereignty remained in force nevertheless. Meanwhile, the proslavery people of western Missouri, the so-called "border ruffians," had invaded Kansas, set up a constitutional convention, made a constitution of an extreme pro-slavery type, the "Lecompton Constitution," refused to submit it fairly to a vote of the people of Kansas, and then referred it to Congress for acceptance,—seeking thus to accomplish the admission of Kansas as a slave State. Had Douglas supported such a scheme, he would have lost all foothold in the North. In the name of popular sovereignty he loudly declared his opposition to the acceptance of any constitution not sanctioned by a formal popular vote. He "did not care," he said, "whether slavery be voted up or down," but there must be a fair vote of the people. Thus he drew upon himself the hostility of the Buchanan administration, which was controlled by the proslavery interest, but he saved his Northern following. More than this, not only did his Democratic admirers now call him "the true champion of freedom," but even some Republicans of large influence, prominent among them Horace Greeley, sympathizing with Douglas in his fight against the Lecompton Constitution, and hoping to detach him permanently from the proslavery interest and to force a lasting breach in the Democratic party, seriously advised the Republicans of Illinois to give up their opposition to Douglas, and to help re-elect him to the Senate. Lincoln was not of that opinion. He believed that great popular movements can succeed only when guided by their faithful friends, and that the antislavery cause could not safely be entrusted to the keeping of one who "did not care whether slavery be voted up or down." This opinion prevailed in Illinois; but the influences within the Republican party over which it prevailed yielded only a reluctant acquiescence, if they acquiesced at all, after having materially strengthened Douglas's position. Such was the situation of things when the campaign of 1858 between Lincoln and Douglas began.

Lincoln opened the campaign on his side at the convention which nominated him as the Republican candidate for the senatorship, with a memorable saying which sounded like a shout from the watchtower of history: "A house divided against itself cannot stand. I believe this government cannot endure permanently half slave and half free. I do not expect the Union to be dissolved. I do not expect the house to fall, but I expect it will cease to be divided. It will become all one thing or all the other. Either the opponents of slavery will arrest the further spread of it, and place it where the public mind shall rest in the belief that it is in the course of ultimate extinction, or its advocates will push it forward, till it shall become alike lawful in all the States,—old as well as new, North as well as South." Then he proceeded to point out that the Nebraska doctrine combined with the Dred Scott decision worked in the direction of making the nation "all slave." Here was the "irrepressible conflict" spoken of by Seward a short time later, in a speech made famous mainly by that phrase. If there was any new discovery in it, the right of priority was Lincoln's. This utterance proved not only his statesmanlike conception of the issue, but also, in his situation as a candidate, the firmness of his moral courage. The friends to whom he had read the draught of this speech before he delivered it warned him anxiously that its delivery might be fatal to his success in the election. This was shrewd advice, in the ordinary sense. While a slaveholder could threaten disunion with impunity, the mere suggestion that the existence of slavery was incompatible with freedom in the Union would hazard the political chances of any public

27

man in the North. But Lincoln was inflexible. "It is true," said he, "and I will deliver it as written.... I would rather be defeated with these expressions in my speech held up and discussed before the people than be victorious without them." The statesman was right in his far-seeing judgment and his conscientious statement of the truth, but the practical politicians were also right in their prediction of the immediate effect. Douglas instantly seized upon the declaration that a house divided against itself cannot stand as the main objective point of his attack, interpreting it as an incitement to a "relentless sectional war," and there is no doubt that the persistent reiteration of this charge served to frighten not a few timid souls.

Lincoln constantly endeavored to bring the moral and philosophical side of the subject to the foreground. "Slavery is wrong" was the keynote of all his speeches. To Douglas's glittering sophism that the right of the people of a Territory to have slavery or not, as they might desire, was in accordance with the principle of true popular sovereignty, he made the pointed answer: "Then true popular sovereignty, according to Senator Douglas, means that, when one man makes another man his slave, no third man shall be allowed to object." To Douglas's argument that the principle which demanded that the people of a Territory should be permitted to choose whether they would have slavery or not "originated when God made man, and placed good and evil before him, allowing him to choose upon his own responsibility," Lincoln solemnly replied: "No; God—did not place good and evil before man, telling him to make his choice. On the contrary, God did tell him there was one tree of the fruit of which he should not eat, upon pain of death." He did not, however, place himself on the most advanced ground taken by the radical anti-slavery men. He admitted that, under the Constitution, "the Southern people were entitled to a Congressional fugitive slave law," although he did not approve the fugitive slave law then existing. He declared also that, if slavery were kept out of the Territories during their territorial existence, as it should be, and if then the people of any Territory, having a fair chance and a clear field, should do such an extraordinary thing as to adopt a slave constitution, uninfluenced by the actual presence of the institution among them, he saw no alternative but to admit such a Territory into the Union. He declared further that, while he should be exceedingly glad to see slavery abolished in the District of Columbia, he would, as a member of Congress, with his present views, not endeavor to bring on that abolition except on condition that emancipation be gradual, that it be approved by the decision of a majority of voters in the District, and that compensation be made to unwilling owners. On every available occasion, he pronounced himself in favor of the deportation and colonization of the blacks, of course with their consent. He repeatedly disavowed any wish on his part to have social and political equality established between whites and blacks. On this point he summed up his views in a reply to Douglas's assertion that the Declaration of Independence, in speaking of all men as being created equal, did not include the negroes, saying: "I do not understand the Declaration of Independence to mean that all men were created equal in all respects. They are not equal in color. But I believe that it does mean to declare that all men are equal in some respects; they are equal in their right to life, liberty, and the pursuit of happiness."

With regard to some of these subjects Lincoln modified his position at a later period, and it has been suggested that he would have professed more advanced principles in his debates with Douglas, had he not feared thereby to lose votes. This view can hardly be sustained. Lincoln had the courage of his opinions, but he was not a radical. The man who risked his election by delivering, against the urgent protest of his friends, the speech about "the house divided against itself" would not have shrunk from the expression of more extreme views, had he really entertained them. It is only fair to assume that he said what at the time he really thought, and that if, subsequently, his opinions changed, it was owing to new conceptions of good policy and of duty brought forth by an entirely new set of circumstances and exigencies. It is characteristic that he continued to adhere to the impracticable colonization plan even after the Emancipation Proclamation had already been issued.

But in this contest Lincoln proved himself not only a debater, but also a political strategist of the first order. The "kind, amiable, and intelligent gentleman," as Douglas had been pleased to call him, was by no means as harmless as a dove. He possessed an uncommon share of that worldly shrewdness which not seldom goes with genuine simplicity of character; and the political experience gathered in the Legislature and in Congress, and in many election campaigns, added to his keen intuitions, had made him as far-sighted a judge of the probable effects of a public man's sayings or doings upon the popular mind, and as accurate a calculator in estimating political chances and forecasting results, as could be found among the party managers in

Illinois. And now he perceived keenly the ugly dilemma in which Douglas found himself, between the Dred Scott decision, which declared the right to hold slaves to exist in the Territories by virtue of the Federal Constitution, and his "great principle of popular sovereignty," according to which the people of a Territory, if they saw fit, were to have the right to exclude slavery therefrom. Douglas was twisting and squirming to the best of his ability to avoid the admission that the two were incompatible. The question then presented itself if it would be good policy for Lincoln to force Douglas to a clear expression of his opinion as to whether, the Dred Scott decision notwithstanding, "the people of a Territory could in any lawful way exclude slavery from its limits prior to the formation of a State constitution." Lincoln foresaw and predicted what Douglas would answer: that slavery could not exist in a Territory unless the people desired it and gave it protection by territorial legislation. In an improvised caucus the policy of pressing the interrogatory on Douglas was discussed. Lincoln's friends unanimously advised against it, because the answer foreseen would sufficiently commend Douglas to the people of Illinois to insure his re-election to the Senate. But Lincoln persisted. "I am after larger game," said he. "If Douglas so answers, he can never be President, and the battle of 1860 is worth a hundred of this." The interrogatory was pressed upon Douglas, and Douglas did answer that, no matter what the decision of the Supreme Court might be on the abstract question, the people of a Territory had the lawful means to introduce or exclude slavery by territorial legislation friendly or unfriendly to the institution. Lincoln found it easy to show the absurdity of the proposition that, if slavery were admitted to exist of right in the Territories by virtue of the supreme law, the Federal Constitution, it could be kept out or expelled by an inferior law, one made by a territorial Legislature. Again the judgment of the politicians, having only the nearest object in view, proved correct: Douglas was reelected to the Senate. But Lincoln's judgment proved correct also: Douglas, by resorting to the expedient of his "unfriendly legislation doctrine," forfeited his last chance of becoming President of the United States. He might have hoped to win, by sufficient atonement, his pardon from the South for his opposition to the Lecompton Constitution; but that he taught the people of the Territories a trick by which they could defeat what the proslavery men considered a constitutional right, and that he called that trick lawful, this the slave power would never forgive. The breach between the

Southern and the Northern Democracy was thenceforth irremediable and fatal.

The Presidential election of 1860 approached. The struggle in Kansas, and the debates in Congress which accompanied it, and which not unfrequently provoked violent outbursts, continually stirred the popular excitement. Within the Democratic party raged the war of factions. The national Democratic convention met at Charleston on the 23d of April, 1860. After a struggle of ten days between the adherents and the opponents of Douglas, during which the delegates from the cotton States had withdrawn, the convention adjourned without having nominated any candidates, to meet again in Baltimore on the 18th of June. There was no prospect, however, of reconciling the hostile elements. It appeared very probable that the Baltimore convention would nominate Douglas, while the seceding Southern Democrats would set up a candidate of their own, representing extreme proslavery principles.

Meanwhile, the national Republican convention assembled at Chicago on the 16th of May, full of enthusiasm and hope. The situation was easily understood. The Democrats would have the South. In order to succeed in the election, the Republicans had to win, in addition to the States carried by Fremont in 1856, those that were classed as "doubtful,"—New Jersey, Pennsylvania, and Indiana, or Illinois in the place of either New Jersey or Indiana. The most eminent Republican statesmen and leaders of the time thought of for the Presidency were Seward and Chase, both regarded as belonging to the more advanced order of antislavery men. Of the two, Seward had the largest following, mainly from New York, New England, and the Northwest. Cautious politicians doubted seriously whether Seward, to whom some phrases in his speeches had undeservedly given the reputation of a reckless radical, would be able to command the whole Republican vote in the doubtful States. Besides, during his long public career he had made enemies. It was evident that those who thought Seward's nomination too hazardous an experiment would consider Chase unavailable for the same reason. They would then look round for an "available" man; and among the "available" men Abraham Lincoln was easily discovered to stand foremost. His great debate with Douglas had given him a national reputation. The people of the East being eager to see the hero of so dramatic a contest, he had been induced to visit several Eastern cities, and had astonished and delighted large and distinguished audiences with speeches of singular power and originality. An address delivered by him in the Cooper Institute in New York, before an audience containing a large number of important persons, was then, and has ever since been, especially praised as one of the most logical and convincing political speeches ever made in this country. The people of the West had grown proud of him as a distinctively Western great man, and his popularity at home had some peculiar features which could be expected to exercise a potent charm. Nor was Lincoln's name as that of an available candidate left to the chance of accidental discovery. It is indeed not probable that he thought of himself as a Presidential possibility, during his contest with Douglas for the senatorship. As late as April, 1859, he had written to a friend who had approached him on the subject that he did not think himself fit for the Presidency. The Vice-Presidency was then the limit of his ambition. But some of his friends in Illinois took the matter seriously in hand, and Lincoln, after some hesitation, then formally authorized "the use of his name." The matter was managed with such energy and excellent judgment that, in the convention, he had not only the whole vote of Illinois to start with, but won votes on all sides without offending any rival. A large majority of the opponents of Seward went over to Abraham Lincoln, and gave him the nomination on the third ballot. As had been foreseen, Douglas was nominated by one wing of the Democratic party at Baltimore, while the extreme proslavery wing put Breckinridge into the field as its candidate. After a campaign conducted with the energy of genuine enthusiasm on the antislavery side the united Republicans defeated the divided Democrats, and Lincoln was elected President by a majority of fifty-seven votes in the electoral colleges.

The result of the election had hardly been declared when the disunion movement in the South, long threatened and carefully planned and prepared, broke out in the shape of open revolt, and nearly a month before Lincoln could be inaugurated as President of the United States seven Southern States had adopted ordinances of secession, formed an independent confederacy, framed a constitution for it, and elected Jefferson Davis its president, expecting the other slaveholding States soon to join them. On the 11th of February, 1861, Lincoln left Springfield for Washington; having, with characteristic simplicity, asked his law partner not to change the sign of the firm "Lincoln and Herndon" during the four years unavoidable absence of the senior partner, and having taken an affectionate and touching leave of his neighbors.

The situation which confronted the new President was appalling: the larger part of the South in open rebellion, the rest of the slaveholding States wavering preparing to follow; the revolt guided by determined, daring, and skillful leaders; the Southern people, apparently full of enthusiasm and military spirit, rushing to arms, some of the forts and arsenals already in their possession; the government of the Union, before the accession of the new President, in the hands of men some of whom actively sympathized with the revolt, while others were hampered by their traditional doctrines in dealing with it, and really gave it aid and comfort by their irresolute attitude; all the departments full of "Southern sympathizers" and honeycombed with disloyalty; the treasury empty, and the public credit at the lowest ebb; the arsenals ill supplied with arms, if not emptied by treacherous practices; the regular army of insignificant strength, dispersed over an immense surface, and deprived of some of its best officers by defection; the navy small and antiquated. But that was not all. The threat of disunion had so often been resorted to by the slave power in years gone by that most Northern people had ceased to believe in its seriousness. But, when disunion actually appeared as a stern reality, something like a chill swept through the whole Northern country. A cry for union and peace at any price rose on all sides. Democratic partisanship reiterated this cry with vociferous vehemence, and even many Republicans grew afraid of the victory they had just achieved at the ballot-box, and spoke of compromise. The country fairly resounded with the noise of "anticoercion meetings." Expressions of firm resolution from determined antislavery men were indeed not wanting, but they were for a while almost drowned by a bewildering confusion of discordant voices. Even this was not all. Potent influences in Europe, with an ill-concealed desire for the permanent disruption of the American Union, eagerly espoused the cause of the Southern seceders, and the two principal maritime powers of the Old World seemed only to be waiting for a favorable opportunity to lend them a helping hand.

This was the state of things to be mastered by "honest Abe Lincoln" when he took his seat in the Presidential chair,—"honest Abe Lincoln," who was so good-natured that he could not say "no"; the greatest achievement in whose life had been a debate on the slavery question; who had never been in any position of power; who was without the slightest experience of high executive duties, and who had only a speaking acquaintance with the men upon whose counsel and cooperation he was to depend. Nor was his accession to power under such circumstances greeted with general confidence even by the members of his party. While he had indeed won much popularity, many Republicans, especially among those who had advocated Seward's nomination for the Presidency, saw the simple "Illinois lawyer" take the reins of government with a feeling little short of dismay. The orators and journals of the opposition were ridiculing and lampooning him without measure. Many people actually wondered how such a man could dare to undertake a task which, as he himself had said to his neighbors in his parting speech, was "more difficult than that of Washington himself had been."

But Lincoln brought to that task, aside from other uncommon qualities, the first requisite,—an intuitive comprehension of its nature. While he did not indulge in the delusion that the Union could be maintained or restored without a conflict of arms, he could indeed not foresee all the problems he would have to solve. He instinctively understood, however, by what means that conflict would have to be conducted by the government of a democracy. He knew that the impending war, whether great or small, would not be like a foreign war, exciting a united national enthusiasm, but a civil war, likely to fan to uncommon heat the animosities of party even in the localities controlled by the government; that this war would have to be carried on not by means of a ready-made machinery, ruled by an undisputed, absolute will, but by means to be furnished by the voluntary action of the people:—armies to be formed by voluntary enlistments; large sums of money to be raised by the people, through representatives, voluntarily taxing themselves; trust of extraordinary power to be voluntarily granted; and war measures, not seldom restricting the rights and liberties to which the citizen was accustomed, to be voluntarily accepted and submitted to by the people, or at least a large majority of them; and that this would have to be kept up not merely during a short period of enthusiastic excitement; but possibly through weary years of alternating success and disaster, hope and despondency. He knew that in order to steer this government by public opinion successfully through all the confusion created by the prejudices and doubts and differences of sentiment distracting the popular mind, and so to propitiate, inspire, mould, organize, unite, and guide the popular will that it might give forth all the means required for the performance of his great task, he would have to take into account all the influences strongly affecting the current of popular thought and feeling, and to direct while appearing to obey.

This was the kind of leadership he intuitively conceived to be needed when a free people were to be led forward en masse to overcome a great common danger under circumstances of appalling difficulty, the leadership which does not dash ahead with brilliant daring, no matter who follows, but which is intent upon rallying all the available forces, gathering in the stragglers, closing up the column, so that the front may advance well supported. For this leadership Abraham Lincoln was admirably fitted, better than any other American statesman of his day; for he understood the plain people, with all their loves and hates, their prejudices and their noble impulses, their weaknesses and their strength, as he understood himself, and his sympathetic nature was apt to draw their sympathy to him.

His inaugural address foreshadowed his official course in characteristic manner. Although yielding nothing in point of principle, it was by no means a flaming antislavery manifesto, such as would have pleased the more ardent Republicans. It was rather the entreaty of a sorrowing father speaking to his wayward children. In the kindliest language he pointed out to the secessionists how ill advised their attempt at disunion was, and why, for their own sakes, they should desist. Almost plaintively, he told them that, while it was not their duty to destroy the Union, it was his sworn duty to preserve it; that the least he could do, under the obligations of his oath, was to possess and hold the property of the United States; that he hoped to do this peaceably; that he abhorred war for any purpose, and that they would have none unless they themselves were the aggressors. It was a masterpiece of persuasiveness, and while Lincoln had accepted many valuable amendments suggested by Seward, it was essentially his own. Probably Lincoln himself did not expect his inaugural address to have any effect upon the secessionists, for he must have known them to be resolved upon disunion at any cost. But it was an appeal to the wavering minds in the North, and upon them it made a profound impression. Every candid man, however timid and halting, had to admit that the President was bound by his oath to do his duty; that under that oath he could do no less than he said he would do; that if the secessionists resisted such an appeal as the President had made, they were bent upon mischief, and that the government must be supported against them. The partisan sympathy with the Southern insurrection which still existed in the North did indeed not disappear, but it diminished perceptibly under the influence of such reasoning. Those who still resisted it did so at the risk of appearing unpatriotic.

It must not be supposed, however, that Lincoln at once succeeded in pleasing everybody, even among his friends,—even among those nearest to him. In selecting his cabinet, which he did substantially before he left Springfield for Washington, he thought it wise to call to his assistance the strong men of his party, especially those who had given evidence of the support they commanded as his competitors in the Chicago convention. In them he found at the same time representatives of the different shades of opinion within the party, and of the different elements—former Whigs and former Democrats— from which the party had recruited itself. This was sound policy under the circumstances. It might indeed have been foreseen that among the members of a cabinet so composed, troublesome disagreements and rivalries would break out. But it was better for the President to have these strong and ambitious men near him as his co-operators than to have them as his critics in Congress, where their differences might have been composed in a common opposition to him. As members of his cabinet he could hope to control them, and to keep them busily employed in the service of a common purpose, if he had the strength to do so. Whether he did possess this strength was soon tested by a singularly rude trial.

There can be no doubt that the foremost members of his cabinet, Seward and Chase, the most eminent Republican statesmen, had felt themselves wronged by their party when in its national convention it preferred to them for the Presidency a man whom, not unnaturally, they thought greatly their inferior in ability and experience as well as in service. The soreness of that disappointment was intensified when they saw this Western man in the White House, with so much of rustic manner and speech as still clung to him, meeting his fellow-citizens, high and low, on a footing of equality, with the simplicity of his good nature unburdened by any conventional dignity of deportment, and dealing with the great business of state in an easy-going, unmethodical, and apparently somewhat irreverent way. They did not understand such a man. Especially Seward, who, as Secretary of State, considered himself next to the Chief Executive, and who quickly accustomed himself to giving orders and making arrangements upon his own motion, thought it necessary that he should rescue the direction of public affairs from hands so unskilled, and take full charge of them himself. At the end of the first month of the administration he submitted a "memorandum" to President Lincoln, which has been first brought to light by Nicolay and Hay, and is one of their most valuable contributions to the history of those days. In that paper Seward actually told the President that at the end of a month's administration the government was still without a policy, either domestic or foreign; that the slavery question should be eliminated from the struggle about the Union; that the matter of the maintenance of the forts and other possessions in the South should be decided with that view; that explanations should be demanded categorically from the governments of Spain and France, which were then preparing, one for the annexation of San Domingo, and both for the invasion of Mexico; that if no satisfactory explanations were received war should be declared against Spain and France by the United States; that explanations should also be sought from Russia and Great Britain, and a vigorous continental spirit of independence against European intervention be aroused all over the American continent; that this policy should be incessantly pursued and directed by somebody; that either the President should devote himself entirely to it, or devolve the direction on some member of his cabinet, whereupon all debate on this policy must end.

This could be understood only as a formal demand that the President should acknowledge his own incompetency to perform his duties, content himself with the amusement of distributing post-offices, and resign his power as to all important affairs into the hands of his Secretary of State. It seems to-day incomprehensible how a statesman of Seward's calibre could at that period conceive a plan of policy in which the slavery question had no place; a policy which rested upon the utterly delusive assumption that the secessionists, who had already formed their Southern Confederacy and were with stern resolution preparing to fight for its independence, could be hoodwinked back into the Union by some sentimental demonstration against European interference; a policy which, at that critical moment, would have involved the Union in a foreign war, thus inviting foreign intervention in favor of the Southern Confederacy, and increasing tenfold its chances in the struggle for independence. But it is equally incomprehensible how Seward could fail to see that this demand of an unconditional surrender was a mortal insult to the head of the government, and that by putting his proposition on paper he delivered himself into the hands of the very man he had insulted; for, had Lincoln, as most Presidents would have done, instantly dismissed

Seward, and published the true reason for that dismissal, it would inevitably have been the end of Seward's career. But Lincoln did what not many of the noblest and greatest men in history would have been noble and great enough to do. He considered that Seward was still capable of rendering great service to his country in the place in which he was, if rightly controlled. He ignored the insult, but firmly established his superiority. In his reply, which he forthwith despatched, he told Seward that the administration had a domestic policy as laid down in the inaugural address with Seward's approval; that it had a foreign policy as traced in Seward's despatches with the President's approval; that if any policy was to be maintained or changed, he, the President, was to direct that on his responsibility; and that in performing that duty the President had a right to the advice of his secretaries. Seward's fantastic schemes of foreign war and continental policies Lincoln brushed aside by passing them over in silence. Nothing more was said. Seward must have felt that he was at the mercy of a superior man; that his offensive proposition had been generously pardoned as a temporary aberration of a great mind, and that he could atone for it only by devoted personal loyalty. This he did. He was thoroughly subdued, and thenceforth submitted to Lincoln his despatches for revision and amendment without a murmur. The war with European nations was no longer thought of; the slavery question found in due time its proper place in the struggle for the Union; and when, at a later period, the dismissal of Seward was demanded by dissatisfied senators, who attributed to him the shortcomings of the administration, Lincoln stood stoutly by his faithful Secretary of State.

Chase, the Secretary of the Treasury, a man of superb presence, of eminent ability and ardent patriotism, of great natural dignity and a certain outward coldness of manner, which made him appear more difficult of approach than he really was, did not permit his disappointment to burst out in such extravagant demonstrations. But Lincoln's ways were so essentially different from his that they never became quite intelligible, and certainly not congenial to him. It might, perhaps, have been better had there been, at the beginning of the administration, some decided clash between Lincoln and Chase, as there was between Lincoln and Seward, to bring on a full mutual explanation, and to make Chase appreciate the real seriousness of Lincoln's nature. But, as it was, their relations always remained somewhat formal, and Chase never felt quite at ease under a chief whom he could not understand, and whose character and powers he never learned to esteem at their true value. At the same time, he devoted himself zealously to the duties of his department, and did the country arduous service under circumstances of extreme difficulty. Nobody recognized this more heartily than Lincoln himself, and they managed to work together until near the end of Lincoln's first Presidential term, when Chase, after some disagreements concerning appointments to office, resigned from the treasury; and, after Taney's death, the President made him Chief Justice.

The rest of the cabinet consisted of men of less eminence, who subordinated themselves more easily. In January, 1862, Lincoln found it necessary to bow Cameron out of the war office, and to put in his place Edwin M. Stanton, a man of intensely practical mind, vehement impulses, fierce positiveness, ruthless energy, immense working power, lofty patriotism, and severest devotion to duty. He accepted the war office not as a partisan, for he had never been a Republican, but only to do all he could in "helping to save the country." The manner in which Lincoln succeeded in taming this lion to his will, by frankly recognizing his great qualities, by giving him the most generous confidence, by aiding him in his work to the full of his power, by kindly concession or affectionate persuasiveness in cases of differing opinions, or, when it was necessary, by firm assertions of superior authority, bears the highest testimony to his skill in the management of men. Stanton, who had entered the service with rather a mean opinion of Lincoln's character and capacity, became one of his warmest, most devoted, and most admiring friends, and with none of his secretaries was Lincoln's intercourse more intimate. To take advice with candid readiness, and to weigh it without any pride of his own opinion, was one of Lincoln's preeminent virtues; but he had not long presided over his cabinet council when his was felt by all its members to be the ruling mind.

The cautious policy foreshadowed in his inaugural address, and pursued during the first period of the civil war, was far from satisfying all his party friends. The ardent spirits among the Union men thought that the whole North should at once be called to arms, to crush the rebellion by one powerful blow. The ardent spirits among the antislavery men insisted that, slavery having brought forth the rebellion, this powerful blow should at once be aimed at slavery. Both complained that the administration was spiritless, undecided, and lamentably slow in its proceedings. Lincoln reasoned otherwise. The ways of thinking and feeling of the masses, of the plain people, were constantly present to his mind. The masses, the plain people, had to furnish the men for the fighting, if fighting was to be done. He believed that the plain people would be ready to fight when it clearly appeared necessary, and that they would feel that necessity when they felt themselves attacked. He therefore waited until the enemies of the Union struck the first blow. As soon as, on the 12th of April, 1861, the first gun was fired in Charleston harbor on the Union flag upon Fort Sumter, the call was sounded, and the Northern people rushed to arms.

Lincoln knew that the plain people were now indeed ready to fight in defence of the Union, but not yet ready to fight for the destruction of slavery. He declared openly that he had a right to summon the people to fight for the Union, but not to summon them to fight for the abolition of slavery as a primary object; and this declaration gave him numberless soldiers for the Union who at that period would have hesitated to do battle against the institution of slavery. For a time he succeeded in rendering harmless the cry of the partisan opposition that the Republican administration were perverting the war for the Union into an "abolition war." But when he went so far as to countermand the acts of some generals in the field, looking to the emancipation of the slaves in the districts covered by their commands, loud complaints arose from earnest antislavery men, who accused the President of turning his back upon the antislavery cause. Many of these antislavery men will now, after a calm retrospect, be willing to admit that it would have been a hazardous policy to endanger, by precipitating a demonstrative fight against slavery, the success of the struggle for the Union.

Lincoln's views and feelings concerning slavery had not changed. Those who conversed with him intimately upon the subject at that period know that he did not expect slavery long to survive the triumph of the Union, even if it were not immediately destroyed by the war. In this he was right. Had the Union armies achieved a decisive victory in an early period of the conflict, and had the seceded States been received back with slavery, the "slave power" would then have been a defeated power, defeated in an attempt to carry out its most effective threat. It would have lost its prestige. Its menaces would have been hollow sound, and ceased to make any one afraid. It could no longer have hoped to expand, to maintain an equilibrium in any branch of Congress, and to control the government. The victorious free States would have largely overbalanced it. It would no longer have been able to withstand the onset of a hostile age. It could no longer have ruled,—

and slavery had to rule in order to live. It would have lingered for a while, but it would surely have been "in the course of ultimate extinction." A prolonged war precipitated the destruction of slavery; a short war might only have prolonged its death struggle. Lincoln saw this clearly; but he saw also that, in a protracted death struggle, it might still have kept disloyal sentiments alive, bred distracting commotions, and caused great mischief to the country. He therefore hoped that slavery would not survive the war.

But the question how he could rightfully employ his power to bring on its speedy destruction was to him not a question of mere sentiment. He himself set forth his reasoning upon it, at a later period, in one of his inimitable letters. "I am naturally antislavery," said he. "If slavery is not wrong, nothing is wrong. I cannot remember the time when I did not so think and feel. And yet I have never understood that the Presidency conferred upon me an unrestricted right to act upon that judgment and feeling. It was in the oath I took that I would, to the best of my ability, preserve, protect, and defend the Constitution of the United States. I could not take the office without taking the oath. Nor was it my view that I might take an oath to get power, and break the oath in using that power. I understood, too, that, in ordinary civil administration, this oath even forbade me practically to indulge my private abstract judgment on the moral question of slavery. I did understand, however, also, that my oath imposed upon me the duty of preserving, to the best of my ability, by every indispensable means, that government, that nation, of which the Constitution was the organic law. I could not feel that, to the best of my ability, I had even tied to preserve the Constitution—if, to save slavery, or any minor matter, I should permit the wreck of government, country, and Constitution all together." In other words, if the salvation of the government, the Constitution, and the Union demanded the destruction of slavery, he felt it to be not only his right, but his sworn duty to destroy it. Its destruction became a necessity of the war for the Union.

As the war dragged on and disaster followed disaster, the sense of that necessity steadily grew upon him. Early in 1862, as some of his friends well remember, he saw, what Seward seemed not to see, that to give the war for the Union an antislavery character was the surest means to prevent the recognition of the Southern Confederacy as an independent nation by European powers; that, slavery being abhorred by the moral sense of civilized mankind, no European government would dare to offer so gross an insult to the public opinion of its

41

people as openly to favor the creation of a state founded upon slavery to the prejudice of an existing nation fighting against slavery. He saw also that slavery untouched was to the rebellion an element of power, and that in order to overcome that power it was necessary to turn it into an element of weakness. Still, he felt no assurance that the plain people were prepared for so radical a measure as the emancipation of the slaves by act of the government, and he anxiously considered that, if they were not, this great step might, by exciting dissension at the North, injure the cause of the Union in one quarter more than it would help it in another. He heartily welcomed an effort made in New York to mould and stimulate public sentiment on the slavery question by public meetings boldly pronouncing for emancipation. At the same time he himself cautiously advanced with a recommendation, expressed in a special message to Congress, that the United States should co-operate with any State which might adopt the gradual abolishment of slavery, giving such State pecuniary aid to compensate the former owners of emancipated slaves. The discussion was started, and spread rapidly. Congress adopted the resolution recommended, and soon went a step farther in passing a bill to abolish slavery in the District of Columbia. The plain people began to look at emancipation on a larger scale as a thing to be considered seriously by patriotic citizens; and soon Lincoln thought that the time was ripe, and that the edict of freedom could be ventured upon without danger of serious confusion in the Union ranks.

The failure of McClellan's movement upon Richmond increased immensely the prestige of the enemy. The need of some great act to stimulate the vitality of the Union cause seemed to grow daily more pressing. On July 21, 1862, Lincoln surprised his cabinet with the draught of a proclamation declaring free the slaves in all the States that should be still in rebellion against the United States on the 1st of January,1863. As to the matter itself he announced that he had fully made up his mind; he invited advice only concerning the form and the time of publication. Seward suggested that the proclamation, if then brought out, amidst disaster and distress, would sound like the last shriek of a perishing cause. Lincoln accepted the suggestion, and the proclamation was postponed. Another defeat followed, the second at Bull Run. But when, after that battle, the Confederate army, under Lee, crossed the Potomac and invaded Maryland, Lincoln vowed in his heart that, if the Union army were now blessed with success, the decree of freedom should surely be issued. The victory of Antietam was won on September 17, and the preliminary Emancipation Proclamation came forth on the a 22d. It was Lincoln's own resolution and act; but practically it bound the nation, and permitted no step backward. In spite of its limitations, it was the actual abolition of slavery. Thus he wrote his name upon the books of history with the title dearest to his heart, the liberator of the slave.

It is true, the great proclamation, which stamped the war as one for "union and freedom," did not at once mark the turning of the tide on the field of military operations. There were more disasters, Fredericksburg and Chancellorsville. But with Gettysburg and Vicksburg the whole aspect of the war changed. Step by step, now more slowly, then more rapidly, but with increasing steadiness, the flag of the Union advanced from field to field toward the final consummation. The decree of emancipation was naturally followed by the enlistment of emancipated negroes in the Union armies. This measure had a anther reaching effect than merely giving the Union armies an increased supply of men. The laboring force of the rebellion was hopelessly disorganized. The war became like a problem of arithmetic. As the Union armies pushed forward, the area from which the Southern Confederacy could draw recruits and supplies constantly grew smaller, while the area from which the Union recruited its strength constantly grew larger; and everywhere, even within the Southern lines, the Union had its allies. The fate of the rebellion was then virtually decided; but it still required much bloody work to convince the brave warriors who fought for it that they were really beaten.

Neither did the Emancipation Proclamation forthwith command universal assent among the people who were loyal to the Union. There were even signs of a reaction against the administration in the fall elections of 1862, seemingly justifying the opinion, entertained by many, that the President had really anticipated the development of popular feeling. The cry that the war for the Union had been turned into an "abolition war" was raised again by the opposition, and more loudly than ever. But the good sense and patriotic instincts of the plain people gradually marshalled themselves on Lincoln's side, and he lost no opportunity to help on this process by personal argument and admonition. There never has been a President in such constant and active contact with the public opinion of the country, as there never has been a President who, while at the head of the government, remained so near to the people. Beyond the circle of those who had long known him the feeling steadily grew that the man in the White House was "honest Abe Lincoln" still, and that every citizen might approach him with complaint, expostulation, or advice, without danger of meeting a rebuff from power-proud authority, or humiliating condescension; and this privilege was used by so many and with such unsparing freedom that only superhuman patience could have endured it all. There are men now living who would to-day read with amazement, if not regret, what they ventured to say or write to him. But Lincoln repelled no one whom he believed to speak to him in good faith and with patriotic purpose. No good advice would go unheeded. No candid criticism would offend him. No honest opposition, while it might pain him, would produce a lasting alienation of feeling between him and the opponent. It may truly be said that few men in power have ever been exposed to more daring attempts to direct their course, to severer censure of their acts, and to more cruel misrepresentation of their motives: And all this he met with that good-natured humor peculiarly his own, and with untiring effort to see the right and to impress it upon those who differed from him. The conversations he had and the correspondence he carried on upon matters of public interest, not only with men in official position, but with private citizens, were almost unceasing, and in a large number of public letters, written ostensibly to meetings, or committees, or persons of importance, he addressed himself directly to the popular mind. Most of these letters stand among the finest monuments of our political literature. Thus he presented the singular spectacle of a President who, in the midst of a great civil war, with unprecedented duties weighing upon him, was constantly in person debating the great features of his policy with the people.

While in this manner he exercised an ever-increasing influence upon the popular understanding, his sympathetic nature endeared him more and more to the popular heart. In vain did journals and speakers of the opposition represent him as a lightminded trifler, who amused himself with frivolous story-telling and coarse jokes, while the blood of the people was flowing in streams. The people knew that the man at the head of affairs, on whose haggard face the twinkle of humor so frequently changed into an expression of profoundest sadness, was more than any other deeply distressed by the suffering he witnessed; that he felt the pain of every wound that was inflicted on the battlefield, and the anguish of every woman or child who had lost husband or father; that whenever he could he was eager to alleviate sorrow, and that his mercy was never implored in vain. They looked to him as one who was with them and of them in all their hopes and fears, their joys and sorrows, who laughed with them and wept with them; and as his heart was theirs; so their hearts turned to him. His popularity was far different from that of Washington, who was revered with awe, or that of Jackson, the unconquerable hero, for whom party enthusiasm never grew weary of shouting. To Abraham Lincoln the people became bound by a genuine sentimental attachment. It was not a matter of respect, or confidence, or party pride, for this feeling spread far beyond the boundary lines of his party; it was an affair of the heart, independent of mere reasoning. When the soldiers in the field or their folks at home spoke of "Father Abraham," there was no cant in it. They felt that their President was really caring for them as a father would, and that they could go to him, every one of them, as they would go to a father, and talk to him of what troubled them, sure to find a willing ear and tender sympathy. Thus, their President, and his cause, and his endeavors, and his success gradually became to them almost matters of family concern. And this popularity carried him triumphantly through the Presidential election of 1864, in spite of an opposition within his own party which at first seemed very formidable.

Many of the radical antislavery men were never quite satisfied with Lincoln's ways of meeting the problems of the time. They were very earnest and mostly very able men, who had positive ideas as to "how this rebellion should be put down." They would not recognize the necessity of measuring the steps of the government according to the progress of opinion among the plain people. They criticised Lincoln's cautious management as irresolute, halting, lacking in definite purpose and in energy; he should not have delayed emancipation so long; he should not have confided important commands to men of doubtful views as to slavery; he should have authorized military commanders to set the slaves free as they went on; he dealt too leniently with unsuccessful generals; he should have put down all factious opposition with a strong hand instead of trying to pacify it; he should have given the people accomplished facts instead of arguing with them, and so on. It is true, these criticisms were not always entirely unfounded. Lincoln's policy had, with the virtues of democratic government, some of its weaknesses, which in the presence of pressing exigencies were apt to deprive governmental action of the necessary vigor; and his kindness of heart, his disposition always to respect the feelings of others, frequently made him recoil from anything like severity, even

45

when severity was urgently called for. But many of his radical critics have since then revised their judgment sufficiently to admit that Lincoln's policy was, on the whole, the wisest and safest; that a policy of heroic methods, while it has sometimes accomplished great results, could in a democracy like ours be maintained only by constant success; that it would have quickly broken down under the weight of disaster; that it might have been successful from the start, had the Union, at the beginning of the conflict, had its Grants and Shermans and Sheridans, its Farraguts and Porters, fully matured at the head of its forces; but that, as the great commanders had to be evolved slowly from the developments of the war, constant success could not be counted upon, and it was best to follow a policy which was in friendly contact with the popular force, and therefore more fit to stand trial of misfortune on the battlefield. But at that period they thought differently, and their dissatisfaction with Lincoln's doings was greatly increased by the steps he took toward the reconstruction of rebel States then partially in possession of the Union forces.

In December, 1863, Lincoln issued an amnesty proclamation, offering pardon to all implicated in the rebellion, with certain specified exceptions, on condition of their taking and maintaining an oath to support the Constitution and obey the laws of the United States and the proclamations of the President with regard to slaves; and also promising that when, in any of the rebel States, a number of citizens equal to one tenth of the voters in 1860 should re-establish a state government in conformity with the oath above mentioned, such should be recognized by the Executive as the true government of the State. The proclamation seemed at first to be received with general favor. But soon another scheme of reconstruction, much more stringent in its provisions, was put forward in the House of Representatives by Henry Winter Davis. Benjamin Wade championed it in the Senate. It passed in the closing moments of the session in July, 1864, and Lincoln, instead of making it a law by his signature, embodied the text of it in a proclamation as a plan of reconstruction worthy of being earnestly considered. The differences of opinion concerning this subject had only intensified the feeling against Lincoln which had long been nursed among the radicals, and some of them openly declared their purpose of resisting his re-election to the Presidency. Similar sentiments were manifested by the advanced antislavery men of Missouri, who, in their hot faction-fight with the "conservatives" of that State, had not received from Lincoln the active support they demanded. Still another class of Union men, mainly in the East, gravely shook their heads when considering the question whether Lincoln should be re-elected. They were those who cherished in their minds an ideal of statesmanship and of personal bearing in high office with which, in their opinion, Lincoln's individuality was much out of accord. They were shocked when they heard him cap an argument upon grave affairs of state with a story about "a man out in Sangamon County,"—a story, to be sure, strikingly clinching his point, but sadly lacking in dignity. They could not understand the man who was capable, in opening a cabinet meeting, of reading to his secretaries a funny chapter from a recent book of Artemus Ward, with which in an unoccupied moment he had relieved his care-burdened mind, and who then solemnly informed the executive council that he had vowed in his heart to issue a proclamation emancipating the slaves as soon as God blessed the Union arms with another victory. They were alarmed at the weakness of a President who would indeed resist the urgent remonstrances of statesmen against his policy, but could not resist the prayer of an old woman for the pardon of a soldier who was sentenced to be shot for desertion. Such men, mostly sincere and ardent patriots, not only wished, but earnestly set to work, to prevent Lincoln's renomination. Not a few of them actually believed, in 1863, that, if the national convention of the Union party were held then, Lincoln would not be supported by the delegation of a single State. But when the convention met at Baltimore, in June, 1864, the voice of the people was heard. On the first ballot Lincoln received the votes of the delegations from all the States except Missouri; and even the Missourians turned over their votes to him before the result of the ballot was declared.

But even after his renomination the opposition to Lincoln within the ranks of the Union party did not subside. A convention, called by the dissatisfied radicals in Missouri, and favored by men of a similar way of thinking in other States, had been held already in May, and had nominated as its candidate for the Presidency General Fremont. He, indeed, did not attract a strong following, but opposition movements from different quarters appeared more formidable. Henry Winter Davis and Benjamin Wade assailed Lincoln in a flaming manifesto. Other Union men, of undoubted patriotism and high standing, persuaded themselves, and sought to persuade the people, that Lincoln's renomination was ill advised and dangerous to the Union cause. As the Democrats had put off their convention until the 29th of

August, the Union party had, during the larger part of the summer, no opposing candidate and platform to attack, and the political campaign languished. Neither were the tidings from the theatre of war of a cheering character. The terrible losses suffered by Grant's army in the battles of the Wilderness spread general gloom. Sherman seemed for a while to be in a precarious position before Atlanta. The opposition to Lincoln within the Union party grew louder in its complaints and discouraging predictions. Earnest demands were heard that his candidacy should be withdrawn. Lincoln himself, not knowing how strongly the masses were attached to him, was haunted by dark forebodings of defeat. Then the scene suddenly changed as if by magic.

The Democrats, in their national convention, declared the war a failure, demanded, substantially, peace at any price, and nominated on such a platform General McClellan as their candidate. Their convention had hardly adjourned when the capture of Atlanta gave a new aspect to the military situation. It was like a sun-ray bursting through a dark cloud. The rank and file of the Union party rose with rapidly growing enthusiasm. The song "We are coming, Father Abraham, three hundred thousand strong," resounded all over the land. Long before the decisive day arrived, the result was beyond doubt, and Lincoln was re-elected President by overwhelming majorities. The election over even his severest critics found themselves forced to admit that Lincoln was the only possible candidate for the Union party in 1864, and that neither political combinations nor campaign speeches, nor even victories in the field, were needed to insure his success. The plain people had all the while been satisfied with Abraham Lincoln: they confided in him; they loved him; they felt themselves near to him; they saw personified in him the cause of Union and freedom; and they went to the ballot-box for him in their strength.

The hour of triumph called out the characteristic impulses of his nature. The opposition within the Union party had stung him to the quick. Now he had his opponents before him, baffled and humiliated. Not a moment did he lose to stretch out the hand of friendship to all. "Now that the election is over," he said, in response to a serenade, "may not all, having a common interest, reunite in a common effort to save our common country? For my own part, I have striven, and will strive, to place no obstacle in the way. So long as I have been here I have not willingly planted a thorn in any man's bosom. While I am deeply sensible to the high compliment of a re-election, it adds nothing to my satisfaction that any other man may be pained or disappointed by the result. May I ask those who were with me to join with me in the same spirit toward those who were against me?" This was Abraham Lincoln's character as tested in the furnace of prosperity.

The war was virtually decided, but not yet ended. Sherman was irresistibly carrying the Union flag through the South. Grant had his iron hand upon the ramparts of Richmond. The days of the Confederacy were evidently numbered. Only the last blow remained to be struck. Then Lincoln's second inauguration came, and with it his second inaugural address. Lincoln's famous "Gettysburg speech" has been much and justly admired. But far greater, as well as far more characteristic, was that inaugural in which he poured out the whole devotion and tenderness of his great soul. It had all the solemnity of a father's last admonition and blessing to his children before he lay down to die. These were its closing words: "Fondly do we hope, fervently do we pray, that this mighty scourge of war may speedily pass away. Yet if God wills that it continue until all the wealth piled up by the bondman's two hundred and fifty years of unrequited toil shall be sunk, and until every drop of blood drawn with the lash shall be paid by another drawn with the sword, as was said three thousand years ago, so still it must be said, `The judgments of the Lord are true and righteous altogether.' With malice toward none, with charity for all, with firmness in the right as God gives us to see the right, let us strive to finish the work we are in; to bind up the nation's wounds; to care for him who shall have borne the battle, and for his widow and his orphan; to do all which may achieve and cherish a just and lasting peace among ourselves and with all nations."

This was like a sacred poem. No American President had ever spoken words like these to the American people. America never had a President who found such words in the depth of his heart.

Now followed the closing scenes of the war. The Southern armies fought bravely to the last, but all in vain. Richmond fell. Lincoln himself entered the city on foot, accompanied only by a few officers and a squad of sailors who had rowed him ashore from the flotilla in the James River, a negro picked up on the way serving as a guide. Never had the world seen a more modest conqueror and a more characteristic triumphal procession, no army with banners and drums, only a throng of those who had been slaves, hastily run together, escorting the victorious chief into the capital of the vanquished foe.

We are told that they pressed around him, kissed his hands and his garments, and shouted and danced for joy, while tears ran down the President's care-furrowed cheeks.

A few days more brought the surrender of Lee's army, and peace was assured. The people of the North were wild with joy. Everywhere festive guns were booming, bells pealing, the churches ringing with thanksgivings, and jubilant multitudes thronging the thoroughfares, when suddenly the news flashed over the land that Abraham Lincoln had been murdered. The people were stunned by the blow. Then a wail of sorrow went up such as America had never heard before. Thousands of Northern households grieved as if they had lost their dearest member. Many a Southern man cried out in his heart that his people had been robbed of their best friend in their humiliation and distress, when Abraham Lincoln was struck down. It was as if the tender affection which his countrymen bore him had inspired all nations with a common sentiment. All civilized mankind stood mourning around the coffin of the dead President. Many of those, here and abroad, who not long before had ridiculed and reviled him were among the first to hasten on with their flowers of eulogy, and in that universal chorus of lamentation and praise there was not a voice that did not tremble with genuine emotion. Never since Washington's death had there been such unanimity of judgment as to a man's virtues and greatness; and even Washington's death, although his name was held in greater reverence, did not touch so sympathetic a chord in the people's hearts.

Nor can it be said that this was owing to the tragic character of Lincoln's end. It is true, the death of this gentlest and most merciful of rulers by the hand of a mad fanatic was well apt to exalt him beyond his merits in the estimation of those who loved him, and to make his renown the object of peculiarly tender solicitude. But it is also true that the verdict pronounced upon him in those days has been affected little by time, and that historical inquiry has served rather to increase than to lessen the appreciation of his virtues, his abilities, his services. Giving the fullest measure of credit to his great ministers,—to Seward for his conduct of foreign affairs, to Chase for the management of the finances under terrible difficulties, to Stanton for the performance of his tremendous task as war secretary,—and readily acknowledging that without the skill and fortitude of the great commanders, and the heroism of the soldiers and sailors under them, success could not have been achieved, the historian still finds that Lincoln's judgment and will were by no means governed by those around him; that the most important steps were owing to his initiative; that his was the deciding and directing mind; and that it was pre-eminently he whose sagacity and whose character enlisted for the administration in its struggles the countenance, the sympathy, and the support of the people. It is found, even, that his judgment on military matters was astonishingly acute, and that the advice and instructions he gave to the generals commanding in the field would not seldom have done honor to the ablest of them. History, therefore, without overlooking, or palliating, or excusing any of his shortcomings or mistakes, continues to place him foremost among the saviours of the Union and the liberators of the slave. More than that, it awards to him the merit of having accomplished what but few political philosophers would have recognized as possible,—of leading the republic through four years of furious civil conflict without any serious detriment to its free institutions.

He was, indeed, while President, violently denounced by the opposition as a tyrant and a usurper, for having gone beyond his constitutional powers in authorizing or permitting the temporary suppression of newspapers, and in wantonly suspending the writ of habeas corpus and resorting to arbitrary arrests. Nobody should be blamed who, when such things are done, in good faith and from patriotic motives protests against them. In a republic, arbitrary stretches of power, even when demanded by necessity, should never be permitted to pass without a protest on the one hand, and without an apology on the other. It is well they did not so pass during our civil war. That arbitrary measures were resorted to is true. That they were resorted to most sparingly, and only when the government thought them absolutely required by the safety of the republic, will now hardly be denied. But certain it is that the history of the world does not furnish a single example of a government passing through so tremendous a crisis as our civil war was with so small a record of arbitrary acts, and so little interference with the ordinary course of law outside the field of military operations. No American President ever wielded such power as that which was thrust into Lincoln's hands. It is to be hoped that no American President ever will have to be entrusted with such power again. But no man was ever entrusted with it to whom its seductions were less dangerous than they proved to be to Abraham Lincoln. With scrupulous care he endeavored, even under the most trying circumstances, to remain strictly within the constitutional limitations of his authority; and whenever the boundary became indistinct, or when the dangers of the situation forced him to cross it, he was equally careful to mark his acts as exceptional measures, justifiable only by the imperative necessities of the civil war, so that they might not pass into history as precedents for similar acts in time of peace. It is an unquestionable fact that during the reconstruction period which followed the war, more things were done capable of serving as dangerous precedents than during the war itself. Thus it may truly be said of him not only that under his guidance the republic was saved from disruption and the country was purified of the blot of slavery, but that, during the stormiest and most perilous crisis in our history, he so conducted the government and so wielded his almost dictatorial power as to leave essentially intact our free institutions in all things that concern the rights and liberties of the citizens. He understood well the nature of the problem. In his first message to Congress he defined it in admirably pointed language: "Must a government be of necessity too strong for the liberties of its own people, or too weak to maintain its own existence? Is there in all republics this inherent weakness?" This question he answered in the name of the great American republic, as no man could have answered it better, with a triumphant "No...."

It has been said that Abraham Lincoln died at the right moment for his fame. However that may be, he had, at the time of his death, certainly not exhausted his usefulness to his country. He was probably the only man who could have guided the nation through the perplexities of the reconstruction period in such a manner as to prevent in the work of peace the revival of the passions of the war. He would indeed not have escaped serious controversy as to details of policy; but he could have weathered it far better than any other statesman of his time, for his prestige with the active politicians had been immensely strengthened by his triumphant re-election; and, what is more important, he would have been supported by the confidence of the victorious Northern people that he would do all to secure the safety of the Union and the rights of the emancipated negro, and at the same time by the confidence of the defeated Southern people that nothing would be done by him from motives of vindictiveness, or of unreasoning fanaticism, or of a selfish party spirit. "With malice toward none, with charity for all," the foremost of the victors would have personified in himself the genius of reconciliation.

He might have rendered the country a great service in another direction. A few days after the fall of Richmond, he pointed out to a friend the crowd of office-seekers besieging his door. "Look at that," said he. "Now we have conquered the rebellion, but here you see something that may become more dangerous to this republic than the rebellion itself." It is true, Lincoln as President did not profess what we now call civil service reform principles. He used the patronage of the government in many cases avowedly to reward party work, in many others to form combinations and to produce political effects advantageous to the Union cause, and in still others simply to put the right man into the right place. But in his endeavors to strengthen the Union cause, and in his search for able and useful men for public duties, he frequently went beyond the limits of his party, and gradually accustomed himself to the thought that, while party service had its value, considerations of the public interest were, as to appointments to office, of far greater consequence. Moreover, there had been such a mingling of different political elements in support of the Union during the civil war that Lincoln, standing at the head of that temporarily united motley mass, hardly felt himself, in the narrow sense of the term, a party man. And as he became strongly impressed with the dangers brought upon the republic by the use of public offices as party spoils, it is by no means improbable that, had he survived the all-absorbing crisis and found time to turn to other objects, one of the most important reforms of later days would have been pioneered by his powerful authority. This was not to be. But the measure of his achievements was full enough for immortality.

To the younger generation Abraham Lincoln has already become a half-mythical figure, which, in the haze of historic distance, grows to more and more heroic proportions, but also loses in distinctness of outline and feature. This is indeed the common lot of popular heroes; but the Lincoln legend will be more than ordinarily apt to become fanciful, as his individuality, assembling seemingly incongruous qualities and forces in a character at the same time grand and most lovable, was so unique, and his career so abounding in startling contrasts. As the state of society in which Abraham Lincoln grew up passes away, the world will read with increasing wonder of the man who, not only of the humblest origin, but remaining the simplest and most unpretending of citizens, was raised to a position of power unprecedented in our history; who was the gentlest and most peace-loving of mortals, unable to see any creature suffer without a pang in his own breast, and suddenly found himself called to conduct the greatest and bloodiest of our wars; who wielded the power of government when stern resolution and relentless force were the order of the day and then won and ruled the popular mind and heart by the tender sympathies of his nature; who was a cautious conservative by temperament and mental habit, and led the most sudden and sweeping social revolution of our time; who, preserving his homely speech and rustic manner even in the most conspicuous position of that period, drew upon himself the scoffs of polite society, and then thrilled the soul of mankind with utterances of wonderful beauty and grandeur; who, in his heart the best friend of the defeated South, was murdered because a crazy fanatic took him for its most cruel enemy; who, while in power, was beyond measure lampooned and maligned by sectional passion and an excited party spirit, and around whose bier friend and foe gathered to praise him which they have since never ceased to do— as one of the greatest of Americans and the best of men.

ABRAHAM LINCOLN, BY JOSEPH H. CHOATE

[This Address was delivered before the Edinburgh Philosophical Institution, November 13, 1900. It is included in this set with the courteous permission of the author and of Messrs. Thomas Y. Crowell & Company.]

ABRAHAM LINCOLN.

When you asked me to deliver the Inaugural Address on this occasion, I recognized that I owed this compliment to the fact that I was the official representative of America, and in selecting a subject I ventured to think that I might interest you for an hour in a brief study in popular government, as illustrated by the life of the most American of all Americans. I therefore offer no apology for asking your attention to Abraham Lincoln—to his unique character and the part he bore in two important achievements of modern history: the preservation of the integrity of the American Union and the emancipation of the colored race.

During his brief term of power he was probably the object of more abuse, vilification, and ridicule than any other man in the world; but when he fell by the hand of an assassin, at the very moment of his stupendous victory, all the nations of the earth vied with one another in paying homage to his character, and the thirty-five years that have since elapsed have established his place in history as one of the great benefactors not of his own country alone, but of the human race.

One of many noble utterances upon the occasion of his death was that in which 'Punch' made its magnanimous recantation of the spirit with which it had pursued him:

"Beside this corpse that bears for winding sheet
The stars and stripes he lived to rear anew,
Between the mourners at his head and feet,
Say, scurrile jester, is there room for you?

....

"Yes, he had lived to shame me from my sneer,
To lame my pencil, and confute my pen
To make me own this hind—of princes peer,
This rail-splitter—a true born king of men."

Fiction can furnish no match for the romance of his life, and biography will be searched in vain for such startling vicissitudes of fortune, so great power and glory won out of such humble beginnings and adverse circumstances.

Doubtless you are all familiar with the salient points of his extraordinary career. In the zenith of his fame he was the wise, patient, courageous, successful ruler of men; exercising more power than any monarch of his time, not for himself, but for the good of the people who had placed it in his hands; commander-in-chief of a vast military power, which waged with ultimate success the greatest war of the century; the triumphant champion of popular government, the deliverer of four millions of his fellowmen from bondage; honored by mankind as Statesman, President, and Liberator.

Let us glance now at the first half of the brief life of which this was the glorious and happy consummation. Nothing could be more squalid and miserable than the home in which Abraham Lincoln was born—a one-roomed cabin without floor or window in what was then the wilderness of Kentucky, in the heart of that frontier life which swiftly moved westward from the Alleghanies to the Mississippi, always in advance of schools and churches, of books and money, of railroads and newspapers, of all things which are generally regarded as the comforts and even necessaries of life. His father, ignorant, needy, and thriftless, content if he could keep soul and body together for himself and his family, was ever seeking, without success, to better his unhappy condition by moving on from one such scene of dreary desolation to another. The rude society which surrounded them was not much better. The struggle for existence was hard, and absorbed all their energies. They were fighting the forest, the wild beast, and the retreating savage. From the time when he could barely handle tools until he attained his majority, Lincoln's life was that of a simple farm laborer, poorly clad, housed, and fed, at work either on his father's wretched farm or hired out to neighboring farmers. But in spite, or perhaps by means, of this rude environment, he grew to be a stalwart giant, reaching six feet four at nineteen, and fabulous stories are told of his feats of strength. With the growth of this mighty frame began that strange education which in his ripening years was to qualify him for the great destiny that awaited him, and the development of those mental faculties and moral endowments which, by the time he reached middle life, were to make him the sagacious, patient, and triumphant leader of a great nation in the crisis of its fate. His whole schooling, obtained during such odd times as could be spared from grinding labor, did not amount in all to as much as one year, and the quality of the teaching was of the lowest possible grade, including only the elements of reading, writing, and ciphering. But out of these simple elements, when rightly used by the right man, education is achieved, and Lincoln knew how to use them. As so often happens, he seemed to take warning from his father's unfortunate example. Untiring industry, an insatiable thirst for knowledge, and an ever-growing desire to rise above his surroundings, were early manifestations of his character.

Books were almost unknown in that community, but the Bible was in every house, and somehow or other Pilgrim's Progress, AEsop's Fables, a History of the United States, and a Life of Washington fell into his hands. He trudged on foot many miles through the wilderness to borrow an English Grammar, and is said to have devoured greedily the contents of the Statutes of Indiana that fell in his way. These few volumes he read and reread—and his power of assimilation was great. To be shut in with a few books and to master them thoroughly sometimes does more for the development of character than freedom to range at large, in a cursory and indiscriminate way, through wide domains of literature. This youth's mind, at any rate, was thoroughly saturated with Biblical knowledge and Biblical language, which, in after life, he used with great readiness and effect. But it was the constant use of the little knowledge which he had that developed and exercised his mental powers. After the hard day's work was done, while others slept, he toiled on, always reading or writing. From an early age he did his own thinking and made up his own mind—invaluable traits in the future President. Paper was such a scarce commodity that, by the evening firelight, he would write and cipher on the back of a wooden shovel, and then shave it off to make room for more. By and by, as he approached manhood, he began speaking in the rude gatherings of the neighborhood, and so laid the foundation of that art of persuading his fellow-men which was one rich result of his education, and one great secret of his subsequent success.

Accustomed as we are in these days of steam and telegraphs to have every intelligent boy survey the whole world each morning before breakfast, and inform himself as to what is going on in every nation, it is hardly possible to conceive how benighted and isolated was the condition of the community at Pigeon Creek in Indiana, of which the family of Lincoln's father formed a part, or how eagerly an ambitious and high-spirited boy, such as he, must have yearned to escape. The first glimpse that he ever got of any world beyond the narrow confines of his home was in 1828, at the age of nineteen, when a neighbor employed him to accompany his son down the river to New Orleans to dispose of a flatboat of produce—a commission which he discharged with great success.

Shortly after his return from this his first excursion into the outer world, his father, tired of failure in Indiana, packed his family and all his worldly goods into a single wagon drawn by two yoke of oxen, and after a fourteen days' tramp through the wilderness, pitched his camp once more, in Illinois. Here Abraham, having come of age and being now his own master, rendered the last service of his minority by ploughing the fifteen-acre lot and splitting from the tall walnut trees of the primeval forest enough rails to surround the little clearing with a fence. Such was the meagre outfit of this coming leader of men, at the age when the future British Prime Minister or statesman emerges from the university as a double first or senior wrangler, with every advantage that high training and broad culture and association with the wisest and the best of men and women can give, and enters upon some form of public service on the road to usefulness and honor, the University course being only the first stage of the public training. So Lincoln, at twenty-one, had just begun his preparation for the public life to which he soon began to aspire. For some years yet he must continue to earn his daily bread by the sweat of his brow, having absolutely no means, no home, no friend to consult. More farm work as a hired hand, a clerkship in a village store, the running of a mill, another trip to New Orleans on a flatboat of his own contriving, a pilot's berth on the river—these were the means by which he subsisted until, in the summer of 1832, when he was twenty-three years of age, an event occurred which gave him public recognition.

The Black Hawk war broke out, and, the Governor of Illinois calling for volunteers to repel the band of savages whose leader bore that name, Lincoln enlisted and was elected captain by his comrades, among whom he had already established his supremacy by signal feats of strength and more than one successful single combat. During the brief hostilities he was engaged in no battle and won no military glory, but his local leadership was established. The same year he offered himself as a candidate for the Legislature of Illinois, but failed at the polls. Yet his vast popularity with those who knew him was manifest. The district consisted of several counties, but the unanimous vote of the people of his own county was for Lincoln. Another unsuccessful attempt at store-keeping was followed by better luck at surveying, until his horse and instruments were levied upon under execution for the debts of his business adventure.

I have been thus detailed in sketching his early years because upon these strange foundations the structure of his great fame and service was built. In the place of a school and university training fortune substituted these trials, hardships, and struggles as a preparation for the great work which he had to do. It turned out to be exactly what the emergency required. Ten years instead at the public school and the university certainly never could have fitted this man for the unique work which was to be thrown upon him. Some other Moses would have had to lead us to our Jordan, to the sight of our promised land of liberty.

At the age of twenty-five he became a member of the Legislature of Illinois, and so continued for eight years, and, in the meantime, qualified himself by reading such law books as he could borrow at random—for he was too poor to buy any to be called to the Bar. For his second quarter of a century—during which a single term in Congress introduced him into the arena of national questions—he gave himself up to law and politics. In spite of his soaring ambition, his two years in Congress gave him no premonition of the great destiny that awaited him,—and at its close, in 1849, we find him an unsuccessful applicant to the President for appointment as Commissioner of the General Land Office—a purely administrative bureau; a fortunate escape for himself and for his country. Year by year his knowledge and power, his experience and reputation extended, and his mental faculties seemed to grow by what they fed on. His power of persuasion, which had always been marked, was developed to an extraordinary degree, now that he became engaged in congenial questions and subjects. Little by little he rose to prominence at the Bar, and became the most effective public speaker in the West. Not that he possessed any of the graces of the orator; but his logic was invincible, and his clearness and force of statement impressed upon his hearers the convictions of his honest mind, while his broad sympathies and sparkling and genial humor made him a universal favorite as far and as fast as his acquaintance extended.

These twenty years that elapsed from the time of his establishment as a lawyer and legislator in Springfield, the new capital of Illinois, furnished a fitting theatre for the development and display of his great faculties, and, with his new and enlarged opportunities, he obviously grew in mental stature in this second period of his career, as if to compensate for the absolute lack of advantages under which he had suffered in youth. As his powers enlarged, his reputation extended, for he was always before the people, felt a warm sympathy with all that concerned them, took a zealous part in the discussion of every public question, and made his personal influence ever more widely and deeply felt.

My brethren of the legal profession will naturally ask me, how could this rough backwoodsman, whose youth had been spent in the forest or on the farm and the flatboat, without culture or training, education or study, by the random reading, on the wing, of a few miscellaneous law books, become a learned and accomplished lawyer? Well, he never did. He never would have earned his salt as a 'Writer' for the 'Signet', nor have won a place as advocate in the Court of Session, where the technique of the profession has reached its highest perfection, and centuries of learning and precedent are involved in the equipment of a lawyer. Dr. Holmes, when asked by an anxious young mother, "When should the education of a child begin?" replied, "Madam, at least two centuries before it is born!" and so I am sure it is with the Scots lawyer.

But not so in Illinois in 1840. Between 1830 and 1880 its population increased twenty-fold, and when Lincoln began practising law in Springfield in 1837, life in Illinois was very crude and simple, and so were the courts and the administration of justice. Books and libraries were scarce. But the people loved justice, upheld the law, and followed the courts, and soon found their favorites among the advocates. The fundamental principles of the common law, as set forth by Blackstone and Chitty, were not so difficult to acquire; and brains, common sense, force of character, tenacity of purpose, ready wit and power of speech did the rest, and supplied all the deficiencies of learning.

The lawsuits of those days were extremely simple, and the principles of natural justice were mainly relied on to dispose of them at the Bar and on the Bench, without resort to technical learning. Railroads, corporations absorbing the chief business of the community, combined and inherited wealth, with all the subtle and intricate questions they breed, had not yet come in—and so the professional agents and the equipment which they require were not needed. But there were many highly educated and powerful men at the Bar of Illinois, even in those early days, whom the spirit of enterprise had carried there in search of fame and fortune. It was by constant contact and conflict with these that Lincoln acquired professional strength and skill. Every community and every age creates its own Bar, entirely adequate for its present uses and necessities. So in Illinois, as the population and wealth of the State kept on doubling and quadrupling, its Bar presented a growing abundance of learning and science and technical skill. The early practitioners grew with its growth and mastered the requisite knowledge. Chicago soon grew to be one of the largest and richest and certainly the most intensely active city on the continent, and if any of my professional friends here had gone there in Lincoln's later years, to try or argue a cause, or transact other business, with any idea that Edinburgh or London had a monopoly of legal learning, science, or subtlety, they would certainly have found their mistake.

In those early days in the West, every lawyer, especially every court lawyer, was necessarily a politician, constantly engaged in the public discussion of the many questions evolved from the rapid development of town, county, State, and Federal affairs. Then and there, in this regard, public discussion supplied the place which the universal activity of the press has since monopolized, and the public speaker who, by clearness, force, earnestness, and wit; could make himself felt on the questions of the day would rapidly come to the front. In the absence of that immense variety of popular entertainments which now feed the public taste and appetite, the people found their chief amusement in frequenting the courts and public and political assemblies. In either place, he who impressed, entertained, and amused them most was the hero of the hour. They did not discriminate very carefully between the eloquence of the forum and the eloquence of the hustings. Human nature ruled in both alike, and he who was the most effective speaker in a political harangue was often retained as most likely to win in a cause to be tried or argued. And I have no doubt in this way many retainers came to Lincoln. Fees, money in any form, had no charms for him—in his eager pursuit of fame he could not afford to make money. He was ambitious to distinguish himself by some great service to mankind, and this ambition for fame and real public service left no room for avarice in his composition. However much he earned, he seems to have ended every year hardly richer than he began it, and yet, as the years passed, fees came to him freely. One of L 1,000 is recorded—a very large professional fee at that time, even in any part of America, the paradise of lawyers. I lay great stress on Lincoln's career as a lawyer—much more than his biographers do because in America a state of things exists wholly different from that which prevails in Great Britain. The profession of the law always has been and is to this day the principal avenue to public life; and I am sure that his training and experience in the courts had much to do with the development of those forces of intellect and character which he soon displayed on a broader arena.

It was in political controversy, of course, that he acquired his wide reputation, and made his deep and lasting impression upon the people of what had now become the powerful State of Illinois, and upon the people of the Great West, to whom the political power and control of the United States were already surely and swiftly passing from the older Eastern States. It was this reputation and this impression, and the familiar knowledge of his character which had come to them from his local leadership, that happily inspired the people of the West to present him as their candidate, and to press him upon the Republican convention of 1860 as the fit and necessary leader in the struggle for life which was before the nation.

That struggle, as you all know, arose out of the terrible question of slavery—and I must trust to your general knowledge of the history of that question to make intelligible the attitude and leadership of Lincoln as the champion of the hosts of freedom in the final contest. Negro slavery had been firmly established in the Southern States from an early period of their history. In 1619, the year before the Mayflower landed our Pilgrim Fathers upon Plymouth Rock, a Dutch ship had discharged a cargo of African slaves at Jamestown in Virginia: All through the colonial period their importation had continued. A few had found their way into the Northern States, but none of them in sufficient numbers to constitute danger or to afford a basis for political power. At the time of the adoption of the Federal Constitution, there is no doubt that the principal members of the convention not only condemned slavery as a moral, social, and political evil, but believed that by the suppression of the slave trade it was in the course of gradual extinction in the South, as it certainly was in the North. Washington, in his will, provided for the emancipation of his own slaves, and said to Jefferson that it "was among his first wishes to see some plan adopted by which slavery in his country might be abolished." Jefferson said, referring to the institution: "I tremble for my country when I think that God is just; that His justice cannot sleep forever,"—and Franklin, Adams, Hamilton, and Patrick Henry were all utterly opposed to it. But it was made the subject of a fatal compromise in the Federal Constitution, whereby its existence was recognized in the States as a basis of representation, the prohibition of the importation of slaves was postponed for twenty years, and the return of fugitive slaves provided for. But no imminent danger was apprehended from it till, by the invention of the cotton gin in 1792, cotton culture by negro labor became at once and forever the leading industry of the South, and gave a new impetus to the importation of slaves, so that in 1808, when the constitutional prohibition took effect, their numbers had vastly increased. From that time forward slavery became the basis of a great political power, and the Southern States, under all circumstances and at every opportunity, carried on a brave and unrelenting struggle for its maintenance and extension.

The conscience of the North was slow to rise against it, though bitter controversies from time to time took place. The Southern leaders threatened disunion if their demands were not complied with. To save the Union, compromise after compromise was made, but each one in the end was broken. The Missouri Compromise, made in 1820 upon the occasion of the admission of Missouri into the Union as a slave State, whereby, in consideration of such admission, slavery was forever excluded from the Northwest Territory, was ruthlessly repealed in 1854, by a Congress elected in the interests of the slave power, the intent being to force slavery into that vast territory which had so long been dedicated to freedom. This challenge at last aroused the slumbering conscience and passion of the North, and led to the formation of the Republican party for the avowed purpose of preventing, by constitutional methods, the further extension of slavery.

In its first campaign, in 1856, though it failed to elect its candidates; it received a surprising vote and carried many of the States. No one could any longer doubt that the North had made up its mind that no threats of disunion should deter it from pressing its cherished purpose and performing its long neglected duty. From the outset, Lincoln was one of the most active and effective leaders and speakers of the new party, and the great debates between Lincoln and Douglas in 1858, as the respective champions of the restriction and extension of slavery, attracted the attention of the whole country. Lincoln's powerful arguments carried conviction everywhere. His moral nature was thoroughly aroused his conscience was stirred to the quick. Unless slavery was wrong, nothing was wrong. Was each man, of whatever color, entitled to the fruits of his own labor, or could one man live in idle luxury by the sweat of another's brow, whose skin was darker? He was an implicit believer in that principle of the Declaration of Independence that all men are vested with certain inalienable rights the equal rights to life, liberty, and the pursuit of happiness. On this doctrine he staked his case and carried it. We have time only for one or two sentences in which he struck the keynote of the contest.

"The real issue in this country is the eternal struggle between these two principles—right and wrong—throughout the world. They are the two principles that have stood face to face from the beginning of time, and will ever continue to struggle. The one is the common right of humanity, and the other the divine right of kings. It is the same principle in whatever shape it develops itself. It is the same spirit that says, 'You work and toil and earn bread and I'll eat it.'"

He foresaw with unerring vision that the conflict was inevitable and irrepressible—that one or the other, the right or the wrong, freedom or slavery, must ultimately prevail and wholly prevail, throughout the country; and this was the principle that carried the war, once begun, to a finish.

One sentence of his is immortal:

"Under the operation of the policy of compromise, the slavery agitation has not only not ceased, but has constantly augmented. In my opinion it will not cease until a crisis shall have been reached and passed. 'A house divided against itself cannot stand.' I believe this government cannot endure permanently half slave and half free. I do not expect the Union to be dissolved. I do not expect the house to fall, but I do expect it will cease to be divided. It will become all one thing or all the other; either the opponents of slavery will arrest the further spread of it, and place it where the public mind shall rest in the belief that it is in the course of ultimate extinction, or its advocates will push it forward till it shall become alike lawful in all the States, old as well as new, North as well as South."

During the entire decade from 1850 to 1860 the agitation of the slavery question was at the boiling point, and events which have become historical continually indicated the near approach of the overwhelming storm. No sooner had the Compromise Acts of 1850 resulted in a temporary peace, which everybody said must be final and perpetual, than new outbreaks came. The forcible carrying away of fugitive slaves by Federal troops from Boston agitated that ancient stronghold of freedom to its foundations. The publication of Uncle Tom's Cabin, which truly exposed the frightful possibilities of the slave system; the reckless attempts by force and fraud to establish it in Kansas against the will of the vast majority of the settlers; the beating of Summer in the Senate Chamber for words spoken in debate; the Dred Scott decision in the Supreme Court, which made the nation realize that the slave power had at last reached the fountain of Federal justice; and finally the execution of John Brown, for his wild raid into Virginia, to invite the slaves to rally to the standard of freedom which he unfurled:—all these events tend to illustrate and confirm Lincoln's contention that the nation could not permanently continue half slave and half free, but must become all one thing or all the other. When John Brown lay under sentence of death he declared that now he was sure that slavery must be wiped out in blood; but neither he nor his executioners dreamt that within four years a million soldiers would be marching across the country for its final extirpation, to the music of the war-song of the great conflict:

    "John Brown's body lies a-mouldering in the grave,
    But his soul is marching on."

And now, at the age of fifty-one, this child of the wilderness, this farm laborer, rail-sputter, flatboatman, this surveyor, lawyer, orator, statesman, and patriot, found himself elected by the great party which was pledged to prevent at all hazards the further extension of slavery, as the chief magistrate of the Republic, bound to carry out that purpose, to be the leader and ruler of the nation in its most trying hour.

Those who believe that there is a living Providence that overrules and conducts the affairs of nations, find in the elevation of this plain man to this extraordinary fortune and to this great duty, which he so fitly discharged, a signal vindication of their faith. Perhaps to this philosophical institution the judgment of our philosopher Emerson will commend itself as a just estimate of Lincoln's historical place.

"His occupying the chair of state was a triumph of the good sense of mankind and of the public conscience. He grew according to the need; his mind mastered the problem of the day: and as the problem grew, so did his comprehension of it. In the war there was no place for holiday magistrate, nor fair-weather sailor. The new pilot was hurried to the helm in a tornado. In four years—four years of battle days—his endurance, his fertility of resource, his magnanimity, were sorely tried, and never found wanting. There, by his courage, his justice, his even temper, his fertile counsel, his humanity, he stood a heroic figure in the centre of a heroic epoch. He is the true history of the American people in his time, the true representative of this continent—father of his country, the pulse of twenty millions throbbing in his heart, the thought of their mind—articulated in his tongue."

He was born great, as distinguished from those who achieve greatness or have it thrust upon them, and his inherent capacity, mental, moral, and physical, having been recognized by the educated intelligence of a free people, they happily chose him for their ruler in a day of deadly peril.

It is now forty years since I first saw and heard Abraham Lincoln, but the impression which he left on my mind is ineffaceable. After his great successes in the West he came to New York to make a political address. He appeared in every sense of the word like one of the plain people among whom he loved to be counted. At first sight there was nothing impressive or imposing about him—except that his great stature singled him out from the crowd: his clothes hung awkwardly on his giant frame; his face was of a dark pallor, without the slightest tinge of color; his seamed and rugged features bore the furrows of hardship and struggle; his deep-set eyes looked sad and anxious; his countenance in repose gave little evidence of that brain power which had raised him from the lowest to the highest station among his countrymen; as he talked to me before the meeting, he seemed ill at ease, with that sort of apprehension which a young man might feel before presenting himself to a new and strange audience, whose critical disposition he dreaded. It was a great audience, including all the noted men—all the learned and cultured of his party in New York editors, clergymen, statesmen, lawyers, merchants, critics. They were all very curious to hear him. His fame as a powerful speaker had preceded him, and exaggerated rumor of his wit—the worst forerunner of an orator—had reached the East. When Mr. Bryant presented him, on the high platform of the Cooper Institute, a vast sea of eager upturned faces greeted him, full of intense curiosity to see what this rude child of the people was like. He was equal to the occasion. When he spoke he was transformed; his eye kindled, his voice rang, his face shone and seemed to light up the whole assembly. For an hour and a half he held his audience in the hollow of his hand. His style of speech and manner of delivery were severely simple. What Lowell called "the grand simplicities of the Bible," with which he was so familiar, were reflected in his discourse. With no attempt at ornament or rhetoric, without parade or pretence, he spoke straight to the point. If any came expecting the turgid eloquence or the ribaldry of the frontier, they must have been startled at the earnest and sincere purity of his utterances. It was marvellous to see how this untutored man, by mere self-discipline and the chastening of his own spirit, had outgrown all meretricious arts, and found his own way to the grandeur and strength of absolute simplicity.

He spoke upon the theme which he had mastered so thoroughly. He demonstrated by copious historical proofs and masterly logic that the fathers who created the Constitution in order to form a more perfect union, to establish justice, and to secure the blessings of liberty to themselves and their posterity, intended to empower the Federal Government to exclude slavery from the Territories. In the kindliest spirit he protested against the avowed threat of the Southern States to destroy the Union if, in order to secure freedom in those vast regions out of which future States were to be carved, a Republican President were elected. He closed with an appeal to his audience, spoken with all the fire of his aroused and kindling conscience, with a full outpouring of his love of justice and liberty, to maintain their political purpose on that lofty and unassailable issue of right and wrong which alone could justify it, and not to be intimidated from their high resolve and sacred duty by any threats of destruction to the government or of ruin to themselves. He concluded with this telling sentence, which drove the whole argument home to all our hearts: "Let us have faith that right makes might, and in that faith let us to the end dare to do our duty as we understand it." That night the great hall, and the next day the whole city, rang with delighted applause and congratulations, and he who had come as a stranger departed with the laurels of great triumph.

Alas! in five years from that exulting night I saw him again, for the last time, in the same city, borne in his coffin through its draped streets. With tears and lamentations a heart-broken people accompanied him from Washington, the scene of his martyrdom, to his last resting-place in the young city of the West where he had worked his way to fame.

Never was a new ruler in a more desperate plight than Lincoln when he entered office on the fourth of March, 1861, four months after his election, and took his oath to support the Constitution and the Union. The intervening time had been busily employed by the Southern States in carrying out their threat of disunion in the event of his election. As soon as the fact was ascertained, seven of them had seceded and had seized upon the forts, arsenals, navy yards, and other public property of the United States within their boundaries, and were making every preparation for war. In the meantime the retiring President, who had been elected by the slave power, and who thought the seceding States could not lawfully be coerced, had done absolutely nothing. Lincoln found himself, by the Constitution, Commander-in-Chief of the Army and Navy of the United States, but with only a remnant of either at hand. Each was to be created on a great scale out of the unknown resources of a nation untried in war.

In his mild and conciliatory inaugural address, while appealing to the seceding States to return to their allegiance, he avowed his purpose to keep the solemn oath he had taken that day, to see that the laws of the Union were faithfully executed, and to use the troops to recover the forts, navy yards, and other property belonging to the government. It is probable, however, that neither side actually realized that war was inevitable, and that the other was determined to fight, until the assault on Fort Sumter presented the South as the first aggressor and roused the North to use every possible resource to maintain the government and the imperilled Union, and to vindicate the supremacy of the flag over every inch of the territory of the United States. The fact that Lincoln's first proclamation called for only 75,000 troops, to serve for three months, shows how inadequate was even his idea of what the future had in store. But from that moment Lincoln and his loyal supporters never faltered in their purpose. They knew they could win, that it was their duty to win, and that for America the whole hope of the future depended upon their winning; for now by the acts of the seceding States the issue of the election to secure or prevent the extension of slavery—stood transformed into a struggle to preserve or to destroy the Union.

We cannot follow this contest. You know its gigantic proportions; that it lasted four years instead of three months; that in its progress, instead of 75,000 men, more than 2,000,000 were enrolled on the side of the government alone; that the aggregate cost and loss to the nation approximated to 1,000,000,000 pounds sterling, and that not less than 300,000 brave and precious lives were sacrificed on each side. History has recorded how Lincoln bore himself during these four frightful years; that he was the real President, the responsible and actual head of the government, through it all; that he listened to all advice, heard all parties, and then, always realizing his responsibility to God and the nation, decided every great executive question for himself. His absolute honesty had become proverbial long before he was President. "Honest Abe Lincoln" was the name by which he had been known for years. His every act attested it.

In all the grandeur of the vast power that he wielded, he never ceased to be one of the plain people, as he always called them, never lost or impaired his perfect sympathy with them, was always in perfect touch with them and open to their appeals; and here lay the very secret of his personality and of his power, for the people in turn gave him their absolute confidence. His courage, his fortitude, his patience, his hopefulness, were sorely tried but never exhausted.

He was true as steel to his generals, but had frequent occasion to change them, as he found them inadequate. This serious and painful duty rested wholly upon him, and was perhaps his most important function as Commander-in-Chief; but when, at last, he recognized in General Grant the master of the situation, the man who could and would bring the war to a triumphant end, he gave it all over to him and upheld him with all his might. Amid all the pressure and distress that the burdens of office brought upon him, his unfailing sense of humor saved him; probably it made it possible for him to live under the burden. He had always been the great story-teller of the West, and he used and cultivated this faculty to relieve the weight of the load he bore.

It enabled him to keep the wonderful record of never having lost his temper, no matter what agony he had to bear. A whole night might be spent in recounting the stories of his wit, humor, and harmless sarcasm. But I will recall only two of his sayings, both about General Grant, who always found plenty of enemies and critics to urge the President to oust him from his command. One, I am sure, will interest all Scotchmen. They repeated with malicious intent the gossip that Grant drank. "What does he drink?" asked Lincoln. "Whiskey," was, of course, the answer; doubtless you can guess the brand. "Well," said the President, "just find out what particular kind he uses and I'll send a barrel to each of my other generals." The other must be as pleasing to the British as to the American ear. When pressed again on other grounds to get rid of Grant, he declared, "I can't spare that man, he fights!"

He was tender-hearted to a fault, and never could resist the appeals of wives and mothers of soldiers who had got into trouble and were under sentence of death for their offences. His Secretary of War and other officials complained that they never could get deserters shot. As surely as the women of the culprit's family could get at him he always gave way. Certainly you will all appreciate his exquisite sympathy with the suffering relatives of those who had fallen in battle. His heart bled with theirs. Never was there a more gentle and tender utterance than his letter to a mother who had given all her sons to her country, written at a time when the angel of death had visited almost every household in the land, and was already hovering over him.

"I have been shown," he says, "in the files of the War Department a statement that you are the mother of five sons who have died gloriously on the field of battle. I feel how weak and fruitless must be any words of mine which should attempt to beguile you from your grief for a loss so overwhelming but I cannot refrain from tendering to you the consolation which may be found in the thanks of the Republic they died to save. I pray that our Heavenly Father may assuage the anguish of your bereavement and leave you only the cherished memory of the loved and the lost, and the solemn pride that must be yours to have laid so costly a sacrifice upon the altar of freedom."

Hardly could your illustrious sovereign, from the depths of her queenly and womanly heart, have spoken words more touching and tender to soothe the stricken mothers of her own soldiers.

The Emancipation Proclamation, with which Mr. Lincoln delighted the country and the world on the first of January, 1863, will doubtless secure for him a foremost place in history among the philanthropists and benefactors of the race, as it rescued, from hopeless and degrading slavery, so many millions of his fellow-beings described in the law and existing in fact as "chattels-personal, in the hands of their owners and possessors, to all intents, constructions, and purposes whatsoever." Rarely does the happy fortune come to one man to render such a service to his kind—to proclaim liberty throughout the land unto all the inhabitants thereof.

Ideas rule the world, and never was there a more signal instance of this triumph of an idea than here. William Lloyd Garrison, who thirty years before had begun his crusade for the abolition of slavery, and had lived to see this glorious and unexpected consummation of the hopeless cause to which he had devoted his life, well described the proclamation as a "great historic event, sublime in its magnitude, momentous and beneficent in its far-reaching consequences, and eminently just and right alike to the oppressor and the oppressed."

Lincoln had always been heart and soul opposed to slavery. Tradition says that on the trip on the flatboat to New Orleans he formed his first and last opinion of slavery at the sight of negroes chained and scourged, and that then and there the iron entered into his soul. No boy could grow to manhood in those days as a poor white in Kentucky and Indiana, in close contact with slavery or in its neighborhood, without a growing consciousness of its blighting effects on free labor, as well as of its frightful injustice and cruelty. In the Legislature of Illinois, where the public sentiment was all for upholding the institution and violently against every movement for its abolition or restriction, upon the passage of resolutions to that effect he had the courage with one companion to put on record his protest, "believing that the institution of slavery is founded both in injustice and bad policy." No great demonstration of courage, you will say; but that was at a time when Garrison, for his abolition utterances, had been dragged by an angry mob through the streets of Boston with a rope around his body, and in the very year that Lovejoy in the same State of Illinois was slain by rioters while defending his press, from which he had printed antislavery appeals.

In Congress he brought in a bill for gradual abolition in the District of Columbia, with compensation to the owners, for until they raised treasonable hands against the life of the nation he always maintained that the property of the slaveholders, into which they had come by two centuries of descent, without fault on their part, ought not to be taken away from them without just compensation. He used to say that, one way or another, he had voted forty-two times for the Wilmot Proviso,

70

which Mr. Wilmot of Pennsylvania moved as an addition to every bill which affected United States territory, "that neither slavery nor involuntary servitude shall ever exist in any part of the said territory," and it is evident that his condemnation of the system, on moral grounds as a crime against the human race, and on political grounds as a cancer that was sapping the vitals of the nation, and must master its whole being or be itself extirpated, grew steadily upon him until it culminated in his great speeches in the Illinois debate.

By the mere election of Lincoln to the Presidency, the further extension of slavery into the Territories was rendered forever impossible—Vox populi, vox Dei. Revolutions never go backward, and when founded on a great moral sentiment stirring the heart of an indignant people their edicts are irresistible and final. Had the slave power acquiesced in that election, had the Southern States remained under the Constitution and within the Union, and relied upon their constitutional and legal rights, their favorite institution, immoral as it was, blighting and fatal as it was, might have endured for another century. The great party that had elected him, unalterably determined against its extension, was nevertheless pledged not to interfere with its continuance in the States where it already existed. Of course, when new regions were forever closed against it, from its very nature it must have begun to shrink and to dwindle; and probably gradual and compensated emancipation, which appealed very strongly to the new President's sense of justice and expediency, would, in the progress of time, by a reversion to the ideas of the founders of the Republic, have found a safe outlet for both masters and slaves. But whom the gods wish to destroy they first make mad, and when seven States, afterwards increased to eleven, openly seceded from the Union, when they declared and began the war upon the nation, and challenged its mighty power to the desperate and protracted struggle for its life, and for the maintenance of its authority as a nation over its territory, they gave to Lincoln and to freedom the sublime opportunity of history.

In his first inaugural address, when as yet not a drop of precious blood had been shed, while he held out to them the olive branch in one hand, in the other he presented the guarantees of the Constitution, and after reciting the emphatic resolution of the convention that nominated him, that the maintenance inviolate of the "rights of the States, and especially the right of each State to order and control its own domestic institutions according to its own judgment exclusively, is essential to that balance of power on which the perfection and endurance of our political fabric depend," he reiterated this sentiment, and declared, with no mental reservation, "that all the protection which, consistently with the Constitution and the laws, can be given, will be cheerfully given to all the States when lawfully demanded for whatever cause as cheerfully to one section as to another."

When, however, these magnanimous overtures for peace and reunion were rejected; when the seceding States defied the Constitution and every clause and principle of it; when they persisted in staying out of the Union from which they had seceded, and proceeded to carve out of its territory a new and hostile empire based on slavery; when they flew at the throat of the nation and plunged it into the bloodiest war of the nineteenth century the tables were turned, and the belief gradually came to the mind of the President that if the Rebellion was not soon subdued by force of arms, if the war must be fought out to the bitter end, then to reach that end the salvation of the nation itself might require the destruction of slavery wherever it existed; that if the war was to continue on one side for Disunion, for no other purpose than to preserve slavery, it must continue on the other side for the Union, to destroy slavery.

As he said, "Events control me; I cannot control events," and as the dreadful war progressed and became more deadly and dangerous, the unalterable conviction was forced upon him that, in order that the frightful sacrifice of life and treasure on both sides might not be all in vain, it had become his duty as Commander-in-Chief of the Army, as a necessary war measure, to strike a blow at the Rebellion which, all others failing, would inevitably lead to its annihilation, by annihilating the very thing for which it was contending. His own words are the best:

"I understood that my oath to preserve the Constitution to the best of my ability imposed upon me the duty of preserving by every indispensable means that government—that nation—of which that Constitution was the organic law. Was it possible to lose the nation and yet preserve the Constitution? By general law, life and limb must be protected, yet often a limb must be amputated to save a life; but a life is never wisely given to save a limb. I felt that measures otherwise unconstitutional might become lawful by becoming indispensable to the preservation of the Constitution through the preservation of the nation. Right or wrong, I assumed this ground and now avow it. I could not feel that to the best of my ability I had ever tried to preserve the Constitution if to save slavery or any minor matter I should permit the wreck of government, country, and Constitution all together."

And so, at last, when in his judgment the indispensable necessity had come, he struck the fatal blow, and signed the proclamation which has made his name immortal. By it, the President, as Commander-in-Chief in time of actual armed rebellion, and as a fit and necessary war measure for suppressing the rebellion, proclaimed all persons held as slaves in the States and parts of States then in rebellion to be thenceforward free, and declared that the executive, with the army and navy, would recognize and maintain their freedom.

In the other great steps of the government, which led to the triumphant prosecution of the war, he necessarily shared the responsibility and the credit with the great statesmen who stayed up his hands in his cabinet, with Seward, Chase and Stanton, and the rest,—and with his generals and admirals, his soldiers and sailors, but this great act was absolutely his own. The conception and execution were exclusively his. He laid it before his cabinet as a measure on which his mind was made up and could not be changed, asking them only for suggestions as to details. He chose the time and the circumstances under which the Emancipation should be proclaimed and when it should take effect.

It came not an hour too soon; but public opinion in the North would not have sustained it earlier. In the first eighteen months of the war its ravages had extended from the Atlantic to beyond the Mississippi. Many victories in the West had been balanced and paralyzed by inaction and disasters in Virginia, only partially redeemed by the bloody and indecisive battle of Antietam; a reaction had set in from the general enthusiasm which had swept the Northern States after the assault upon Sumter. It could not truly be said that they had lost heart, but faction was raising its head. Heard through the land like the blast of a bugle, the proclamation rallied the patriotism of the country to fresh sacrifices and renewed ardor. It was a step that could not be revoked. It relieved the conscience of the nation from an incubus that had oppressed it from its birth. The United States were rescued from the false predicament in which they had been from the beginning, and the great popular heart leaped with new enthusiasm for "Liberty and Union, henceforth and forever, one and inseparable." It brought not only moral but material support to the cause of the government, for within two years 120,000 colored troops were enlisted in the military service and following the national flag, supported by all

73

the loyalty of the North, and led by its choicest spirits. One mother said, when her son was offered the command of the first colored regiment, "If he accepts it I shall be as proud as if I had heard that he was shot." He was shot heading a gallant charge of his regiment.... The Confederates replied to a request of his friends for his body that they had "buried him under a layer of his niggers...;" but that mother has lived to enjoy thirty-six years of his glory, and Boston has erected its noblest monument to his memory.

The effect of the proclamation upon the actual progress of the war was not immediate, but wherever the Federal armies advanced they carried freedom with them, and when the summer came round the new spirit and force which had animated the heart of the government and people were manifest. In the first week of July the decisive battle of Gettysburg turned the tide of war, and the fall of Vicksburg made the great river free from its source to the Gulf.

On foreign nations the influence of the proclamation and of these new victories was of great importance. In those days, when there was no cable, it was not easy for foreign observers to appreciate what was really going on; they could not see clearly the true state of affairs, as in the last year of the nineteenth century we have been able, by our new electric vision, to watch every event at the antipodes and observe its effect. The Rebel emissaries, sent over to solicit intervention, spared no pains to impress upon the minds of public and private men and upon the press their own views of the character of the contest. The prospects of the Confederacy were always better abroad than at home. The stock markets of the world gambled upon its chances, and its bonds at one time were high in favor.

Such ideas as these were seriously held: that the North was fighting for empire and the South for independence; that the Southern States, instead of being the grossest oligarchies, essentially despotisms, founded on the right of one man to appropriate the fruit of other men's toil and to exclude them from equal rights, were real republics, feebler to be sure than their Northern rivals, but representing the same idea of freedom, and that the mighty strength of the nation was being put forth to crush them; that Jefferson Davis and the Southern leaders had created a nation; that the republican experiment had failed and the Union had ceased to exist. But the crowning argument to foreign minds was that it was an utter impossibility for the government to win in the contest; that the success of the Southern States, so far as separation was concerned, was as certain as any event yet future and contingent could be; that the subjugation of the South by the North, even if it could be accomplished, would prove a calamity to the United States and the world, and especially calamitous to the negro race; and that such a victory would necessarily leave the people of the South for many generations cherishing deadly hostility against the government and the North, and plotting always to recover their independence.

When Lincoln issued his proclamation he knew that all these ideas were founded in error; that the national resources were inexhaustible; that the government could and would win, and that if slavery were once finally disposed of, the only cause of difference being out of the way, the North and South would come together again, and by and by be as good friends as ever. In many quarters abroad the proclamation was welcomed with enthusiasm by the friends of America; but I think the demonstrations in its favor that brought more gladness to Lincoln's heart than any other were the meetings held in the manufacturing centres, by the very operatives upon whom the war bore the hardest, expressing the most enthusiastic sympathy with the proclamation, while they bore with heroic fortitude the grievous privations which the war entailed upon them. Mr. Lincoln's expectation when he announced to the world that all slaves in all States then in rebellion were set free must have been that the avowed position of his government, that the continuance of the war now meant the annihilation of slavery, would make intervention impossible for any foreign nation whose people were lovers of liberty—and so the result proved.

The growth and development of Lincoln's mental power and moral force, of his intense and magnetic personality, after the vast responsibilities of government were thrown upon him at the age of fifty-two, furnish a rare and striking illustration of the marvellous capacity and adaptability of the human intellect—of the sound mind in the sound body. He came to the discharge of the great duties of the Presidency with absolutely no experience in the administration of government, or of the vastly varied and complicated questions of foreign and domestic policy which immediately arose, and continued to press upon him during the rest of his life; but he mastered each as it came, apparently with the facility of a trained and experienced ruler. As Clarendon said of Cromwell, "His parts seemed to be raised by the demands of great station." His life through it all was one of intense labor, anxiety, and distress, without one hour of peaceful repose from first to last. But he rose to every occasion. He led public opinion, but did not march so far in advance of it as to fail of its effective support in every great emergency. He knew the heart and thought of the people, as no man not in constant and absolute sympathy with them could have known it, and so holding their confidence, he triumphed through and with them. Not only was there this steady growth of intellect, but the infinite delicacy of his nature and its capacity for refinement developed also, as exhibited in the purity and perfection of his language and style of speech. The rough backwoodsman, who had never seen the inside of a university, became in the end, by self-training and the exercise of his own powers of mind, heart, and soul, a master of style, and some of his utterances will rank with the best, the most perfectly adapted to the occasion which produced them.

Have you time to listen to his two-minutes speech at Gettysburg, at the dedication of the Soldiers' Cemetery? His whole soul was in it:

"Four score and seven years ago our fathers brought forth on this continent a new nation, conceived in liberty and dedicated to the proposition that all men are created equal. Now we are engaged in a great civil war, testing whether that nation, or any nation so conceived and so dedicated, can long endure. We are met on a great battlefield of that war. We have come to dedicate a portion of that field as a final resting-place for those who here gave their lives that that nation might live. It is altogether fitting and proper that we should do this. But in a larger sense we cannot dedicate—we cannot consecrate—we cannot hallow this ground. The brave men, living and dead, who struggled here have consecrated it far above our poor power to add or detract. The world will little note, nor long remember, what we say here but it can never forget what they did here. It is for us, the living, rather, to be dedicated here to the unfinished work which they who fought here have thus far so nobly advanced. It is rather for us to be here dedicated to the great task remaining before us that from these honored dead we take increased devotion to that cause for which they gave the last full measure of devotion—that we here highly resolve that these dead shall not have died in vain—that this nation under God shall have a new birth of freedom—and that government of the people, by the people, and for the people shall not perish from the earth."

He lived to see his work indorsed by an overwhelming majority of his countrymen. In his second inaugural address, pronounced just forty days before his death, there is a single passage which well displays his indomitable will and at the same time his deep religious feeling, his sublime charity to the enemies of his country, and his broad and catholic humanity:

"If we shall suppose that American slavery is one of those offences which in the Providence of God must needs come, but which, having continued through the appointed time, He now wills to remove, and that He gives to both North and South this terrible war, as the woe due to those by whom the offence came, shall we discern therein any departure from those divine attributes which the believers in a living God always ascribe to Him? Fondly do we hope, fervently do we pray, that this mighty scourge of war may speedily pass away. Yet, if God wills that it continue until all the wealth piled by the bondsmen's two hundred and fifty years of unrequited toil shall be sunk, and until every drop of blood drawn with the lash shall be paid with another drawn by the sword, as was said three thousand years ago, so still it must be said, 'the judgments of the Lord are true and righteous altogether.'

"With malice toward none, with charity for all, with firmness in the right as God gives us to see the right let us strive on to finish the work we are in to bind up the nation's wounds; to care for him who shall have borne the battle and for his widow and his orphan to do all which may achieve, and cherish a just and lasting peace among ourselves, and with all nations."

His prayer was answered. The forty days of life that remained to him were crowned with great historic events. He lived to see his Proclamation of Emancipation embodied in an amendment of the Constitution, adopted by Congress, and submitted to the States for ratification. The mighty scourge of war did speedily pass away, for it was given him to witness the surrender of the Rebel army and the fall of their capital, and the starry flag that he loved waving in triumph over the national soil. When he died by the madman's hand in the supreme hour of victory, the vanquished lost their best friend, and the human race one of its noblest examples; and all the friends of freedom and justice, in whose cause he lived and died, joined hands as mourners at his grave.

THE WRITINGS OF ABRAHAM LINCOLN, 1832-1843

1832

ADDRESS TO THE PEOPLE OF SANGAMON COUNTY. March 9, 1832.

FELLOW CITIZENS:—Having become a candidate for the honorable office of one of your Representatives in the next General Assembly of this State, in according with an established custom and the principles of true Republicanism it becomes my duty to make known to you, the people whom I propose to represent, my sentiments with regard to local affairs.

Time and experience have verified to a demonstration the public utility of internal improvements. That the poorest and most thinly populated countries would be greatly benefited by the opening of good roads, and in the clearing of navigable streams within their limits, is what no person will deny. Yet it is folly to undertake works of this or any other without first knowing that we are able to finish them—as half-finished work generally proves to be labor lost. There cannot justly be any objection to having railroads and canals, any more than to other good things, provided they cost nothing. The only objection is to paying for them; and the objection arises from the want of ability to pay.

With respect to the County of Sangamon, some....

Yet, however desirable an object the construction of a railroad through our country may be, however high our imaginations may be heated at thoughts of it,—there is always a heart-appalling shock accompanying the amount of its cost, which forces us to shrink from our pleasing anticipations. The probable cost of this contemplated railroad is estimated at $290,000; the bare statement of which, in my opinion, is sufficient to justify the belief that the improvement of the

Sangamon River is an object much better suited to our infant resources.......

What the cost of this work would be, I am unable to say. It is probable, however, that it would not be greater than is common to streams of the same length. Finally, I believe the improvement of the Sangamon River to be vastly important and highly desirable to the people of the county; and, if elected, any measure in the Legislature having this for its object, which may appear judicious, will meet my approbation and receive my support.

It appears that the practice of loaning money at exorbitant rates of interest has already been opened as a field for discussion; so I suppose I may enter upon it without claiming the honor or risking the danger which may await its first explorer. It seems as though we are never to have an end to this baneful and corroding system, acting almost as prejudicially to the general interests of the community as a direct tax of several thousand dollars annually laid on each county for the benefit of a few individuals only, unless there be a law made fixing the limits of usury. A law for this purpose, I am of opinion, may be made without materially injuring any class of people. In cases of extreme necessity, there could always be means found to cheat the law; while in all other cases it would have its intended effect. I would favor the passage of a law on this subject which might not be very easily evaded. Let it be such that the labor and difficulty of evading it could only be justified in cases of greatest necessity.

Upon the subject of education, not presuming to dictate any plan or system respecting it, I can only say that I view it as the most important subject which we as a people can be engaged in. That every man may receive at least a moderate education, and thereby be enabled to read the histories of his own and other countries, by which he may duly appreciate the value of our free institutions, appears to be an object of vital importance, even on this account alone, to say nothing of the advantages and satisfaction to be derived from all being able to read the Scriptures, and other works both of a religious and moral nature, for themselves.

For my part, I desire to see the time when education—and by its means, morality, sobriety, enterprise, and industry—shall become much more general than at present, and should be gratified to have it in my power to contribute something to the advancement of any measure which might have a tendency to accelerate that happy period.

With regard to existing laws, some alterations are thought to be necessary. Many respectable men have suggested that our estray laws, the law respecting the issuing of executions, the road law, and some others, are deficient in their present form, and require alterations. But, considering the great probability that the framers of those laws were wiser than myself, I should prefer not meddling with them, unless they were first attacked by others; in which case I should feel it both a privilege and a duty to take that stand which, in my view, might tend most to the advancement of justice.

But, fellow-citizens, I shall conclude. Considering the great degree of modesty which should always attend youth, it is probable I have already been more presuming than becomes me. However, upon the subjects of which I have treated, I have spoken as I have thought. I may be wrong in regard to any or all of them; but, holding it a sound maxim that it is better only sometimes to be right than at all times to be wrong, so soon as I discover my opinions to be erroneous, I shall be ready to renounce them.

Every man is said to have his peculiar ambition. Whether it be true or not, I can say, for one, that I have no other so great as that of being truly esteemed of my fellow-men, by rendering myself worthy of their esteem. How far I shall succeed in gratifying this ambition is yet to be developed. I am young, and unknown to many of you. I was born, and have ever remained, in the most humble walks of life. I have no wealthy or popular relations or friends to recommend me. My case is thrown exclusively upon the independent voters of the county; and, if elected, they will have conferred a favor upon me for which I shall be unremitting in my labors to compensate. But, if the good people in their wisdom shall see fit to keep me in the background, I have been too familiar with disappointments to be very much chagrined.

Your friend and fellow-citizen, A. LINCOLN.

New Salem, March 9, 1832.

1833

TO E. C. BLANKENSHIP.
NEW SALEM, Aug. 10, 1833
E. C. BLANKENSHIP.

Dear Sir:—In regard to the time David Rankin served the enclosed discharge shows correctly—as well as I can recollect—having no writing to refer. The transfer of Rankin from my company occurred as follows: Rankin having lost his horse at Dixon's ferry and having acquaintance in one of the foot companies who were going down the river was desirous to go with them, and one Galishen being an acquaintance of mine and belonging to the company in which Rankin wished to go wished to leave it and join mine, this being the case it was agreed that they should exchange places and answer to each other's names—as it was expected we all would be discharged in very few days. As to a blanket—I have no knowledge of Rankin ever getting any. The above embraces all the facts now in my recollection which are pertinent to the case.

I shall take pleasure in giving any further information in my power should you call on me.

Your friend, A. LINCOLN.

RESPONSE TO REQUEST FOR POSTAGE RECEIPT TO Mr. SPEARS.

Mr. SPEARS:

At your request I send you a receipt for the postage on your paper. I am somewhat surprised at your request. I will, however, comply with it. The law requires newspaper postage to be paid in advance, and now that I have waited a full year you choose to wound my feelings by insinuating that unless you get a receipt I will probably make you pay it again.

Respectfully, A. LINCOLN.

1836

ANNOUNCEMENT OF POLITICAL VIEWS.
New Salem, June 13, 1836.

TO THE EDITOR OF THE "JOURNAL"—In your paper of last Saturday I see a communication, over the signature of "Many Voters," in which the candidates who are announced in the Journal are called upon to "show their hands." Agreed. Here's mine.

I go for all sharing the privileges of the government who assist in bearing its burdens. Consequently, I go for admitting all whites to the right of suffrage who pay taxes or bear arms (by no means excluding females).

If elected, I shall consider the whole people of Sangamon my constituents, as well those that oppose as those that support me.

While acting as their representative, I shall be governed by their will on all subjects upon which I have the means of knowing what their will is; and upon all others I shall do what my own judgment teaches me will best advance their interests. Whether elected or not, I go for distributing the proceeds of the sales of the public lands to the several States, to enable our State, in common with others, to dig canals and construct railroads without borrowing money and paying the interest on it. If alive on the first Monday in November, I shall vote for Hugh L. White for President.

Very respectfully, A. LINCOLN.

RESPONSE TO POLITICAL SMEAR
TO ROBERT ALLEN
New Salem, June 21, 1836

DEAR COLONEL:—I am told that during my absence last week you passed through this place, and stated publicly that you were in possession of a fact or facts which, if known to the public, would entirely destroy the prospects of N. W. Edwards and myself at the ensuing election; but that, through favor to us, you should forbear to divulge them. No one has needed favors more than I, and, generally, few have been less unwilling to accept them; but in this case favor to me would be injustice to the public, and therefore I must beg your pardon for declining it. That I once had the confidence of the people of Sangamon, is sufficiently evident; and if I have since done anything, either by design or misadventure, which if known would subject me to a forfeiture of that confidence, he that knows of that thing, and conceals it, is a traitor to his country's interest.

I find myself wholly unable to form any conjecture of what fact or facts, real or supposed, you spoke; but my opinion of your veracity will not permit me for a moment to doubt that you at least believed what you said. I am flattered with the personal regard you manifested for me; but I do hope that, on more mature reflection, you will view the public interest as a paramount consideration, and therefore determine to let the worst come. I here assure you that the candid statement of facts on your part, however low it may sink me, shall never break the tie of personal friendship between us. I wish an answer to this, and you are at liberty to publish both, if you choose.

Very respectfully, A. LINCOLN.

TO MISS MARY OWENS.
VANDALIA, December 13, 1836.

MARY:—I have been sick ever since my arrival, or I should have written sooner. It is but little difference, however, as I have very little even yet to write. And more, the longer I can avoid the mortification of looking in the post-office for your letter and not finding it, the better. You see I am mad about that old letter yet. I don't like very well to risk you again. I'll try you once more, anyhow.

The new State House is not yet finished, and consequently the Legislature is doing little or nothing. The governor delivered an inflammatory political message, and it is expected there will be some sparring between the parties about it as soon as the two Houses get to business. Taylor delivered up his petition for the new county to one of our members this morning. I am told he despairs of its success, on account of all the members from Morgan County opposing it. There are names enough on the petition, I think, to justify the members from our county in going for it; but if the members from Morgan oppose it, which they say they will, the chance will be bad.

Our chance to take the seat of government to Springfield is better than I expected. An internal-improvement convention was held there since we met, which recommended a loan of several millions of dollars, on the faith of the State, to construct railroads. Some of the Legislature are for it, and some against it; which has the majority I cannot tell. There is great strife and struggling for the office of the United States Senator here at this time. It is probable we shall ease their pains in a few days. The opposition men have no candidate of their own, and consequently they will smile as complacently at the angry snarl of the contending Van Buren candidates and their respective friends as the Christian does at Satan's rage. You recollect that I mentioned at the outset of this letter that I had been unwell. That is the fact, though I believe I am about well now; but that, with other things I cannot account for, have conspired, and have gotten my spirits so low that I feel that I would rather be any place in the world than here. I really cannot endure the thought of staying here ten weeks. Write back as soon as you get this, and, if possible, say something that will please me, for really I have not been pleased since I left you. This letter is so dry and stupid that I am ashamed to send it, but with my present feelings I cannot do any better.

Give my best respects to Mr. and Mrs. Able and family.

Your friend, LINCOLN

1837

SPEECH IN ILLINOIS LEGISLATURE.
January [?], 1837

Mr. CHAIRMAN:—Lest I should fall into the too common error of being mistaken in regard to which side I design to be upon, I shall make it my first care to remove all doubt on that point, by declaring that I am opposed to the resolution under consideration, in toto. Before I proceed to the body of the subject, I will further remark, that it is not without a considerable degree of apprehension that I venture to cross the track of the gentleman from Coles [Mr. Linder]. Indeed, I do not believe I could muster a sufficiency of courage to come in contact with that gentleman, were it not for the fact that he, some days since, most graciously condescended to assure us that he would never be found wasting ammunition on small game. On the same fortunate occasion, he further gave us to understand, that he regarded himself as being decidedly the superior of our common friend from Randolph [Mr. Shields]; and feeling, as I really do, that I, to say the most of myself, am nothing more than the peer of our friend from Randolph, I shall regard the gentleman from Coles as decidedly my superior also, and consequently, in the course of what I shall have to say, whenever I shall have occasion to allude to that gentleman, I shall endeavor to adopt that kind of court language which I understand to be due to decided superiority. In one faculty, at least, there can be no dispute of the gentleman's superiority over me and most other men, and that is, the faculty of entangling a subject, so that neither himself, or any other man, can find head or tail to it. Here he has introduced a resolution embracing ninety-nine printed lines across common writing paper, and yet more than one half of his opening speech has been made upon subjects about which there is not one word said in his resolution.

Though his resolution embraces nothing in regard to the constitutionality of the Bank, much of what he has said has been with a view to make the impression that it was unconstitutional in its inception. Now, although I am satisfied that an ample field may be found within the pale of the resolution, at least for small game, yet, as the gentleman has traveled out of it, I feel that I may, with all due humility, venture to follow him. The gentleman has discovered that some gentleman at Washington city has been upon the very eve of deciding our Bank unconstitutional, and that he would probably have completed his very authentic decision, had not some one of the Bank officers placed his hand upon his mouth, and begged him to withhold it. The fact that the individuals composing our Supreme Court have, in an official capacity, decided in favor of the constitutionality of the Bank, would, in my mind, seem a sufficient answer to this. It is a fact known to all, that the members of the Supreme Court, together with the Governor, form a Council of Revision, and that this Council approved this Bank charter. I ask, then, if the extra-judicial decision not quite but almost made by the gentleman at Washington, before whom, by the way, the question of the constitutionality of our Bank never has, nor never can come—is to be taken as paramount to a

85

decision officially made by that tribunal, by which, and which alone, the constitutionality of the Bank can ever be settled? But, aside from this view of the subject, I would ask, if the committee which this resolution proposes to appoint are to examine into the Constitutionality of the Bank? Are they to be clothed with power to send for persons and papers, for this object? And after they have found the bank to be unconstitutional, and decided it so, how are they to enforce their decision? What will their decision amount to? They cannot compel the Bank to cease operations, or to change the course of its operations. What good, then, can their labors result in? Certainly none.

The gentleman asks, if we, without an examination, shall, by giving the State deposits to the Bank, and by taking the stock reserved for the State, legalize its former misconduct. Now I do not pretend to possess sufficient legal knowledge to decide whether a legislative enactment proposing to, and accepting from, the Bank, certain terms, would have the effect to legalize or wipe out its former errors, or not; but I can assure the gentleman, if such should be the effect, he has already got behind the settlement of accounts; for it is well known to all, that the Legislature, at its last session, passed a supplemental Bank charter, which the Bank has since accepted, and which, according to his doctrine, has legalized all the alleged violations of its original charter in the distribution of its stock.

I now proceed to the resolution. By examination it will be found that the first thirty-three lines, being precisely one third of the whole, relate exclusively to the distribution of the stock by the commissioners appointed by the State. Now, Sir, it is clear that no question can arise on this portion of the resolution, except a question between capitalists in regard to the ownership of stock. Some gentlemen have their stock in their hands, while others, who have more money than they know what to do with, want it; and this, and this alone, is the question, to settle which we are called on to squander thousands of the people's money. What interest, let me ask, have the people in the settlement of this question? What difference is it to them whether the stock is owned by Judge Smith or Sam Wiggins? If any gentleman be entitled to stock in the Bank, which he is kept out of possession of by others, let him assert his right in the Supreme Court, and let him or his antagonist, whichever may be found in the wrong, pay the costs of suit. It is an old maxim, and a very sound one, that he that dances should always pay the fiddler. Now, Sir, in the present case, if any gentlemen, whose money is a burden to them, choose to lead off a dance, I am decidedly opposed to the people's money being used to pay the fiddler. No one can doubt that the examination proposed by this resolution must cost the State some ten or twelve thousand dollars; and all this to settle a question in which the people have no interest, and about which they care nothing. These capitalists generally act harmoniously and in concert, to fleece the people, and now that they have got into a quarrel with themselves we are called upon to appropriate the people's money to settle the quarrel.

I leave this part of the resolution and proceed to the remainder. It will be found that no charge in the remaining part of the resolution, if true, amounts to the violation of the Bank charter, except one, which I will notice in due time. It might seem quite sufficient to say no more upon any of these charges or insinuations than enough to show they are not violations of the charter; yet, as they are ingeniously framed and handled, with a view to deceive and mislead, I will notice in their order all the most prominent of them. The first of these is in relation to a connection between our Bank and several banking institutions in other States. Admitting this connection to exist, I should like to see the gentleman from Coles, or any other gentleman, undertake to show that there is any harm in it. What can there be in such a connection, that the people of Illinois are willing to pay their money to get a peep into? By a reference to the tenth section of the Bank charter, any gentleman can see that the framers of the act contemplated the holding of stock in the institutions of other corporations. Why, then, is it, when neither law nor justice forbids it, that we are asked to spend our time and money in inquiring into its truth?

The next charge, in the order of time, is, that some officer, director, clerk or servant of the Bank, has been required to take an oath of secrecy in relation to the affairs of said Bank. Now, I do not know whether this be true or false—neither do I believe any honest man cares. I know that the seventh section of the charter expressly guarantees to the Bank the right of making, under certain restrictions, such by-laws as it may think fit; and I further know that the requiring an oath of secrecy would not transcend those restrictions. What, then, if the Bank has chosen to exercise this right? Whom can it injure? Does not every merchant have his secret mark? and who is ever silly enough to complain of it? I presume if the Bank does require any such oath of secrecy, it is done through a motive of delicacy to those individuals who deal with it. Why, Sir, not many days since, one gentleman upon this floor, who, by the way, I have no doubt is now ready to join this hue and cry against the Bank, indulged in a philippic against one of the Bank officials, because, as he said, he had divulged a secret.

Immediately following this last charge, there are several insinuations in the resolution, which are too silly to require any sort of notice, were it not for the fact that they conclude by saying, "to the great injury of the people at large." In answer to this I would say that it is strange enough, that the people are suffering these "great injuries," and yet are not sensible of it! Singular indeed that the people should be writhing under oppression and injury, and yet not one among them to be found to raise the voice of complaint. If the Bank be inflicting injury upon the people, why is it that not a single petition is presented to this body on the subject? If the Bank really be a grievance, why is it that no one of the real people is found to ask redress of it? The truth is, no such oppression exists. If it did, our people would groan with memorials and petitions, and we would not be permitted to rest day or night, till we had put it down. The people know their rights, and they are never slow to assert and maintain them, when they are invaded. Let them call for an investigation, and I shall ever stand ready to respond to the call. But they have made no such call. I make the assertion boldly, and without fear of contradiction, that no man, who does not hold an office, or does not aspire to one, has ever found any fault of the Bank. It has doubled the prices of the products of their farms, and filled their pockets with a sound circulating medium, and they are all well pleased with its operations. No, Sir, it is the politician who is the first to sound the alarm (which, by the way, is a false one.) It is he, who, by these unholy means, is endeavoring to blow up a storm that he may ride upon and direct. It is he, and he alone, that here proposes to spend thousands of the people's public treasure, for no other advantage to them than to make valueless in their pockets the reward of their industry. Mr. Chairman, this work is exclusively the work of politicians; a set of men who have interests aside from the interests of the people, and who, to say the most of them, are, taken as a mass, at least one long step removed from honest men. I say this with the greater freedom, because, being a politician myself, none can regard it as personal.

Again, it is charged, or rather insinuated, that officers of the Bank have loaned money at usurious rates of interest. Suppose this to be true, are we to send a committee of this House to inquire into it? Suppose the committee should find it true, can they redress the injured individuals? Assuredly not. If any individual had been injured in this way, is there not an ample remedy to be found in the laws of the land? Does the gentleman from Coles know that there is a statute standing in full force making it highly penal for an individual to loan money at a higher rate of interest than twelve per cent? If he does not he is too ignorant to be placed at the head of the committee which his resolution purposes and if he does, his neglect to mention it shows him to be too uncandid to merit the respect or confidence of any one.

But besides all this, if the Bank were struck from existence, could not the owners of the capital still loan it usuriously, as well as now? whatever the Bank, or its officers, may have done, I know that usurious transactions were much more frequent and enormous before the commencement of its operations than they have ever been since.

The next insinuation is, that the Bank has refused specie payments. This, if true is a violation of the charter. But there is not the least probability of its truth; because, if such had been the fact, the individual to whom payment was refused would have had an interest in making it public, by suing for the damages to which the charter entitles him. Yet no such thing has been done; and the strong presumption is, that the insinuation is false and groundless.

From this to the end of the resolution, there is nothing that merits attention—I therefore drop the particular examination of it.

By a general view of the resolution, it will be seen that a principal object of the committee is to examine into, and ferret out, a mass of corruption supposed to have been committed by the commissioners who apportioned the stock of the Bank. I believe it is universally understood and acknowledged that all men will ever act correctly unless they have a motive to do otherwise. If this be true, we can only suppose that the commissioners acted corruptly by also supposing that they were bribed to do so. Taking this view of the subject, I would ask if the Bank is likely to find it more difficult to bribe the committee of seven, which, we are about to appoint, than it may have found it to bribe the commissioners?

(Here Mr. Linder called to order. The Chair decided that Mr. Lincoln was not out of order. Mr. Linder appealed to the House, but, before the question was put, withdrew his appeal, saying he preferred to let the gentleman go on; he thought he would break his own neck. Mr. Lincoln proceeded:)

Another gracious condescension! I acknowledge it with gratitude. I know I was not out of order; and I know every sensible man in the

House knows it. I was not saying that the gentleman from Coles could be bribed, nor, on the other hand, will I say he could not. In that particular I leave him where I found him. I was only endeavoring to show that there was at least as great a probability of any seven members that could be selected from this House being bribed to act corruptly, as there was that the twenty-four commissioners had been so bribed. By a reference to the ninth section of the Bank charter, it will be seen that those commissioners were John Tilson, Robert K. McLaughlin, Daniel Warm, A.G. S. Wight, John C. Riley, W. H. Davidson, Edward M. Wilson, Edward L. Pierson, Robert R. Green, Ezra Baker, Aquilla Wren, John Taylor, Samuel C. Christy, Edmund Roberts, Benjamin Godfrey, Thomas Mather, A. M. Jenkins, W. Linn, W. S. Gilman, Charles Prentice, Richard I. Hamilton, A.H. Buckner, W. F. Thornton, and Edmund D. Taylor.

These are twenty-four of the most respectable men in the State. Probably no twenty-four men could be selected in the State with whom the people are better acquainted, or in whose honor and integrity they would more readily place confidence. And I now repeat, that there is less probability that those men have been bribed and corrupted, than that any seven men, or rather any six men, that could be selected from the members of this House, might be so bribed and corrupted, even though they were headed and led on by "decided superiority" himself.

In all seriousness, I ask every reasonable man, if an issue be joined by these twenty-four commissioners, on the one part, and any other seven men, on the other part, and the whole depend upon the honor and integrity of the contending parties, to which party would the greatest degree of credit be due? Again: Another consideration is, that we have no right to make the examination. What I shall say upon this head I design exclusively for the law-loving and law-abiding part of the House. To those who claim omnipotence for the Legislature, and who in the plenitude of their assumed powers are disposed to disregard the Constitution, law, good faith, moral right, and everything else, I have not a word to say. But to the law-abiding part I say, examine the Bank charter, go examine the Constitution, go examine the acts that the General Assembly of this State has passed, and you will find just as much authority given in each and every of them to compel the Bank to bring its coffers to this hall and to pour their contents upon this floor, as to compel it to submit to this examination which this resolution proposes. Why, Sir, the gentleman from Coles, the mover of this resolution, very lately denied on this floor that the Legislature had any right to repeal or otherwise meddle with its own acts, when those acts were made in the nature of contracts, and had been accepted and acted on by other parties. Now I ask if this resolution does not propose, for this House alone, to do what he, but the other day, denied the right of the whole Legislature to do? He must either abandon the position he then took, or he must now vote against his own resolution. It is no difference to me, and I presume but little to any one else, which he does.

I am by no means the special advocate of the Bank. I have long thought that it would be well for it to report its condition to the General Assembly, and that cases might occur, when it might be proper to make an examination of its affairs by a committee. Accordingly, during the last session, while a bill supplemental to the Bank charter was pending before the House, I offered an amendment to the same, in these words: "The said corporation shall, at the next session of the General Assembly, and at each subsequent General Session, during the existence of its charter, report to the same the amount of debts due from said corporation; the amount of debts due to the same; the amount of specie in its vaults, and an account of all lands then owned by the same, and the amount for which such lands have been taken; and moreover, if said corporation shall at any time neglect or refuse to submit its books, papers, and all and everything necessary for a full and fair examination of its affairs, to any person or persons appointed by the General Assembly, for the purpose of making such examination, the said corporation shall forfeit its charter."

This amendment was negatived by a vote of 34 to 15. Eleven of the 34 who voted against it are now members of this House; and though it would be out of order to call their names, I hope they will all recollect themselves, and not vote for this examination to be made without authority, inasmuch as they refused to receive the authority when it was in their power to do so.

I have said that cases might occur, when an examination might be proper; but I do not believe any such case has now occurred; and if it has, I should still be opposed to making an examination without legal authority. I am opposed to encouraging that lawless and mobocratic spirit, whether in relation to the Bank or anything else, which is already abroad in the land and is spreading with rapid and fearful impetuosity, to the ultimate overthrow of every institution, of every moral principle, in which persons and property have hitherto found security.

But supposing we had the authority, I would ask what good can result from the examination? Can we declare the Bank unconstitutional, and compel it to desist from the abuses of its power, provided we find such abuses to exist? Can we repair the injuries which it may have done to individuals? Most certainly we can do none of these things. Why then shall we spend the public money in such employment? Oh, say the examiners, we can injure the credit of the Bank, if nothing else, Please tell me, gentlemen, who will suffer most by that? You cannot injure, to any extent, the stockholders. They are men of wealth—of large capital; and consequently, beyond the power of malice. But by injuring the credit of the Bank, you will depreciate the value of its paper in the hands of the honest and unsuspecting farmer and mechanic, and that is all you can do. But suppose you could effect your whole purpose; suppose you could wipe the Bank from existence, which is the grand ultimatum of the project, what would be the consequence? why, Sir, we should spend several thousand dollars of the public treasure in the operation, annihilate the currency of the State, render valueless in the hands of our people that reward of their former labors, and finally be once more under the comfortable obligation of paying the Wiggins loan, principal and interest.

OPPOSITION TO MOB-RULE
ADDRESS BEFORE THE YOUNG MEN'S
LYCEUM OF SPRINGFIELD, ILLINOIS.
January 27, 1837.

As a subject for the remarks of the evening, "The Perpetuation of our Political Institutions" is selected.

In the great journal of things happening under the sun, we, the American people, find our account running under date of the nineteenth century of the Christian era. We find ourselves in the peaceful possession of the fairest portion of the earth as regards extent of territory, fertility of soil, and salubrity of climate. We find ourselves under the government of a system of political institutions conducing more essentially to the ends of civil and religious liberty than any of which the history of former times tells us. We, when mounting the stage of existence, found ourselves the legal inheritors of these fundamental blessings. We toiled not in the acquirement or establishment of them; they are a legacy bequeathed us by a once hardy, brave, and patriotic, but now lamented and departed, race of ancestors. Theirs was the task (and nobly they performed it) to possess themselves, and through themselves us, of this goodly land, and to uprear upon its hills and its valleys a political edifice of liberty and equal rights; it is ours only to transmit these—the former unprofaned by the foot of an invader, the latter undecayed by the lapse of time and untorn by usurpation—to the latest generation that fate shall permit the world to know. This task gratitude to our fathers, justice to ourselves, duty to posterity, and love for our species in general, all imperatively require us faithfully to perform.

How then shall we perform it? At what point shall we expect the approach of danger? By what means shall we fortify against it? Shall we expect some transatlantic military giant to step the ocean and crush us at a blow? Never! All the armies of Europe, Asia, and Africa combined, with all the treasure of the earth (our own excepted) in their military chest, with a Bonaparte for a commander, could not by force take a drink from the Ohio or make a track on the Blue Ridge in a trial of a thousand years.

At what point then is the approach of danger to be expected? I answer: If it ever reach us it must spring up amongst us; it cannot come from abroad. If destruction be our lot we must ourselves be its author and finisher. As a nation of freemen we must live through all time, or die by suicide.

I hope I am over-wary; but if I am not, there is even now something of ill omen amongst us. I mean the increasing disregard for law which pervades the country—the growing disposition to substitute the wild and furious passions in lieu of the sober judgment of courts, and the worse than savage mobs for the executive ministers of justice. This disposition is awfully fearful in any community; and that it now exists in ours, though grating to our feelings to admit, it would be a violation of truth and an insult to our intelligence to deny. Accounts of outrages committed by mobs form the everyday news of the times. They have pervaded the country from New England to Louisiana; they are neither peculiar to the eternal snows of the former nor the burning suns of the latter; they are not the creature of climate, neither are they confined to the slave holding or the non-slave holding States. Alike they spring up among the pleasure-hunting masters of Southern slaves,

93

and the order-loving citizens of the land of steady habits. Whatever then their cause may be, it is common to the whole country.

It would be tedious as well as useless to recount the horrors of all of them. Those happening in the State of Mississippi and at St. Louis are perhaps the most dangerous in example and revolting to humanity. In the Mississippi case they first commenced by hanging the regular gamblers—a set of men certainly not following for a livelihood a very useful or very honest occupation, but one which, so far from being forbidden by the laws, was actually licensed by an act of the Legislature passed but a single year before. Next, negroes suspected of conspiring to raise an insurrection were caught up and hanged in all parts of the State; then, white men supposed to be leagued with the negroes; and finally, strangers from neighboring States, going thither on business, were in many instances subjected to the same fate. Thus went on this process of hanging, from gamblers to negroes, from negroes to white citizens, and from these to strangers, till dead men were seen literally dangling from the boughs of trees upon every roadside, and in numbers almost sufficient to rival the native Spanish moss of the country as a drapery of the forest.

Turn then to that horror-striking scene at St. Louis. A single victim only was sacrificed there. This story is very short, and is perhaps the most highly tragic of anything of its length that has ever been witnessed in real life. A mulatto man by the name of McIntosh was seized in the street, dragged to the suburbs of the city, chained to a tree, and actually burned to death; and all within a single hour from the time he had been a freeman attending to his own business and at peace with the world.

Such are the effects of mob law, and such are the scenes becoming more and more frequent in this land so lately famed for love of law and order, and the stories of which have even now grown too familiar to attract anything more than an idle remark.

But you are perhaps ready to ask, "What has this to do with the perpetuation of our political institutions?" I answer, It has much to do with it. Its direct consequences are, comparatively speaking, but a small evil, and much of its danger consists in the proneness of our minds to regard its direct as its only consequences. Abstractly considered, the hanging of the gamblers at Vicksburg was of but little consequence. They constitute a portion of population that is worse than useless in any community; and their death, if no pernicious example be set by it, is never matter of reasonable regret with any one.

94

If they were annually swept from the stage of existence by the plague or smallpox, honest men would perhaps be much profited by the operation. Similar too is the correct reasoning in regard to the burning of the negro at St. Louis. He had forfeited his life by the perpetration of an outrageous murder upon one of the most worthy and respectable citizens of the city, and had he not died as he did, he must have died by the sentence of the law in a very short time afterwards. As to him alone, it was as well the way it was as it could otherwise have been. But the example in either case was fearful. When men take it in their heads to-day to hang gamblers or burn murderers, they should recollect that in the confusion usually attending such transactions they will be as likely to hang or burn some one who is neither a gambler nor a murderer as one who is, and that, acting upon the example they set, the mob of to-morrow may, and probably will, hang or burn some of them by the very same mistake. And not only so: the innocent, those who have ever set their faces against violations of law in every shape, alike with the guilty fall victims to the ravages of mob law; and thus it goes on, step by step, till all the walls erected for the defense of the persons and property of individuals are trodden down and disregarded. But all this, even, is not the full extent of the evil. By such examples, by instances of the perpetrators of such acts going unpunished, the lawless in spirit are encouraged to become lawless in practice; and having been used to no restraint but dread of punishment, they thus become absolutely unrestrained. Having ever regarded government as their deadliest bane, they make a jubilee of the suspension of its operations, and pray for nothing so much as its total annihilation. While, on the other hand, good men, men who love tranquillity, who desire to abide by the laws and enjoy their benefits, who would gladly spill their blood in the defense of their country, seeing their property destroyed, their families insulted, and their lives endangered, their persons injured, and seeing nothing in prospect that forebodes a change for the better, become tired of and disgusted with a government that offers them no protection, and are not much averse to a change in which they imagine they have nothing to lose. Thus, then, by the operation of this mobocratic spirit which all must admit is now abroad in the land, the strongest bulwark of any government, and particularly of those constituted like ours, may effectually be broken down and destroyed—I mean the attachment of the people. Whenever this effect shall be produced among us; whenever the vicious portion of population shall be permitted to gather in bands of hundreds and thousands, and burn churches, ravage and rob provision-stores, throw printing presses into rivers, shoot editors, and hang and burn obnoxious persons at pleasure and with impunity, depend on it, this government cannot last. By such things the feelings of the best citizens will become more or less alienated from it, and thus it will be left without friends, or with too few, and those few too weak to make their friendship effectual. At such a time, and under such circumstances, men of sufficient talent and ambition will not be wanting to seize the opportunity, strike the blow, and overturn that fair fabric which for the last half century has been the fondest hope of the lovers of freedom throughout the world.

I know the American people are much attached to their government; I know they would suffer much for its sake; I know they would endure evils long and patiently before they would ever think of exchanging it for another,—yet, notwithstanding all this, if the laws be continually despised and disregarded, if their rights to be secure in their persons and property are held by no better tenure than the caprice of a mob, the alienation of their affections from the government is the natural consequence; and to that, sooner or later, it must come.

Here, then, is one point at which danger may be expected.

The question recurs, How shall we fortify against it? The answer is simple. Let every American, every lover of liberty, every well-wisher to his posterity swear by the blood of the Revolution never to violate in the least particular the laws of the country, and never to tolerate their violation by others. As the patriots of seventy-six did to the support of the Declaration of Independence, so to the support of the Constitution and laws let every American pledge his life, his property, and his sacred honor. Let every man remember that to violate the law is to trample on the blood of his father, and to tear the charter of his own and his children's liberty. Let reverence for the laws be breathed by every American mother to the lisping babe that prattles on her lap; let it be taught in schools, in seminaries, and in colleges; let it be written in primers, spelling books, and in almanacs; let it be preached from the pulpit, proclaimed in legislative halls, and enforced in courts of justice. And, in short, let it become the political religion of the nation; and let the old and the young, the rich and the poor, the grave and the gay of all sexes and tongues and colors and conditions, sacrifice unceasingly upon its altars.

While ever a state of feeling such as this shall universally or even very generally prevail throughout the nation, vain will be every effort, and fruitless every attempt, to subvert our national freedom.

When, I so pressingly urge a strict observance of all the laws, let me not be understood as saying there are no bad laws, or that grievances may not arise for the redress of which no legal provisions have been made. I mean to say no such thing. But I do mean to say that although bad laws, if they exist, should be repealed as soon as possible, still, while they continue in force, for the sake of example they should be religiously observed. So also in unprovided cases. If such arise, let proper legal provisions be made for them with the least possible delay, but till then let them, if not too intolerable, be borne with.

There is no grievance that is a fit object of redress by mob law. In any case that may arise, as, for instance, the promulgation of abolitionism, one of two positions is necessarily true—that is, the thing is right within itself, and therefore deserves the protection of all law and all good citizens, or it is wrong, and therefore proper to be prohibited by legal enactments; and in neither case is the interposition of mob law either necessary, justifiable, or excusable.

But it may be asked, Why suppose danger to our political institutions? Have we not preserved them for more than fifty years? And why may we not for fifty times as long?

We hope there is no sufficient reason. We hope all danger may be overcome; but to conclude that no danger may ever arise would itself be extremely dangerous. There are now, and will hereafter be, many causes, dangerous in their tendency, which have not existed heretofore, and which are not too insignificant to merit attention. That our government should have been maintained in its original form, from its establishment until now, is not much to be wondered at. It had many props to support it through that period, which now are decayed and crumbled away. Through that period it was felt by all to be an undecided experiment; now it is understood to be a successful one. Then, all that sought celebrity and fame and distinction expected to find them in the success of that experiment. Their all was staked upon it; their destiny was inseparably linked with it. Their ambition aspired to display before an admiring world a practical demonstration of the truth of a proposition which had hitherto been considered at best no better than problematical—namely, the capability of a people to govern themselves. If they succeeded they were to be immortalized;

their names were to be transferred to counties, and cities, and rivers, and mountains; and to be revered and sung, toasted through all time. If they failed, they were to be called knaves and fools, and fanatics for a fleeting hour; then to sink and be forgotten. They succeeded. The experiment is successful, and thousands have won their deathless names in making it so. But the game is caught; and I believe it is true that with the catching end the pleasures of the chase. This field of glory is harvested, and the crop is already appropriated. But new reapers will arise, and they too will seek a field. It is to deny what the history of the world tells us is true, to suppose that men of ambition and talents will not continue to spring up amongst us. And when they do, they will as naturally seek the gratification of their ruling passion as others have done before them. The question then is, Can that gratification be found in supporting and in maintaining an edifice that has been erected by others? Most certainly it cannot. Many great and good men, sufficiently qualified for any task they should undertake, may ever be found whose ambition would aspire to nothing beyond a seat in Congress, a Gubernatorial or a Presidential chair; but such belong not to the family of the lion, or the tribe of the eagle. What! think you these places would satisfy an Alexander, a Caesar, or a Napoleon? Never! Towering genius disdains a beaten path. It seeks regions hitherto unexplored. It sees no distinction in adding story to story upon the monuments of fame erected to the memory of others. It denies that it is glory enough to serve under any chief. It scorns to tread in the footsteps of any predecessor, however illustrious. It thirsts and burns for distinction; and if possible, it will have it, whether at the expense of emancipating slaves or enslaving freemen. Is it unreasonable, then, to expect that some man possessed of the loftiest genius, coupled with ambition sufficient to push it to its utmost stretch, will at some time spring up among us? And when such an one does it will require the people to be united with each other, attached to the government and laws, and generally intelligent, to successfully frustrate his designs.

Distinction will be his paramount object, and although he would as willingly, perhaps more so, acquire it by doing good as harm, yet, that opportunity being past, and nothing left to be done in the way of building up, he would set boldly to the task of pulling down.

Here then is a probable case, highly dangerous, and such an one as could not have well existed heretofore.

Another reason which once was, but which, to the same extent, is now no more, has done much in maintaining our institutions thus far. I mean the powerful influence which the interesting scenes of the Revolution had upon the passions of the people as distinguished from their judgment. By this influence, the jealousy, envy, and avarice incident to our nature, and so common to a state of peace, prosperity, and conscious strength, were for the time in a great measure smothered and rendered inactive, while the deep-rooted principles of hate, and the powerful motive of revenge, instead of being turned against each other, were directed exclusively against the British nation. And thus, from the force of circumstances, the basest principles of our nature were either made to lie dormant, or to become the active agents in the advancement of the noblest of causes—that of establishing and maintaining civil and religious liberty.

But this state of feeling must fade, is fading, has faded, with the circumstances that produced it.

I do not mean to say that the scenes of the Revolution are now or ever will be entirely forgotten, but that, like everything else, they must fade upon the memory of the world, and grow more and more dim by the lapse of time. In history, we hope, they will be read of, and recounted, so long as the Bible shall be read; but even granting that they will, their influence cannot be what it heretofore has been. Even then they cannot be so universally known nor so vividly felt as they were by the generation just gone to rest. At the close of that struggle, nearly every adult male had been a participator in some of its scenes. The consequence was that of those scenes, in the form of a husband, a father, a son, or a brother, a living history was to be found in every family—a history bearing the indubitable testimonies of its own authenticity, in the limbs mangled, in the scars of wounds received, in the midst of the very scenes related—a history, too, that could be read and understood alike by all, the wise and the ignorant, the learned and the unlearned. But those histories are gone. They can be read no more forever. They were a fortress of strength; but what invading foeman could never do the silent artillery of time has done—the leveling of its walls. They are gone. They were a forest of giant oaks; but the all-restless hurricane has swept over them, and left only here and there a lonely trunk, despoiled of its verdure, shorn of its foliage, unshading and unshaded, to murmur in a few more gentle breezes, and to combat with its mutilated limbs a few more ruder storms, then to sink and be no more.

They were pillars of the temple of liberty; and now that they have crumbled away that temple must fall unless we, their descendants, supply their places with other pillars, hewn from the solid quarry of sober reason. Passion has helped us, but can do so no more. It will in future be our enemy. Reason cold, calculating, unimpassioned reason—must furnish all the materials for our future support and defense. Let those materials be moulded into general intelligence, sound morality, and in particular, a reverence for the Constitution and laws; and that we improved to the last, that we remained free to the last, that we revered his name to the last, that during his long sleep we permitted no hostile foot to pass over or desecrate his resting place, shall be that which to learn the last trump shall awaken our Washington.

Upon these let the proud fabric of freedom rest, as the rock of its basis; and as truly as has been said of the only greater institution, "the gates of hell shall not prevail against it."

PROTEST IN THE ILLINOIS LEGISLATURE ON THE SUBJECT OF SLAVERY. March 3, 1837.

The following protest was presented to the House, which was read and ordered to be spread in the journals, to wit:

"Resolutions upon the subject of domestic slavery having passed both branches of the General Assembly at its present session, the undersigned hereby protest against the passage of the same.

"They believe that the institution of slavery is founded on both injustice and bad policy, but that the promulgation of abolition doctrines tends rather to increase than abate its evils.

"They believe that the Congress of the United States has no power under the Constitution to interfere with the institution of slavery in the different States.

"They believe that the Congress of the United States has the power, under the Constitution, to abolish slavery in the District of Columbia, but that the power ought not to be exercised, unless at the request of the people of the District.

"The difference between these opinions and those contained in the said resolutions is their reason for entering this protest.

"DAN STONE,
"A. LINCOLN,
"Representatives from the County of Sangamon."

TO MISS MARY OWENS.
SPRINGFIELD, May 7, 1837.
MISS MARY S. OWENS.

FRIEND MARY:—I have commenced two letters to send you before this, both of which displeased me before I got half done, and so I tore them up. The first I thought was not serious enough, and the second was on the other extreme. I shall send this, turn out as it may.

This thing of living in Springfield is rather a dull business, after all; at least it is so to me. I am quite as lonesome here as I ever was anywhere in my life. I have been spoken to by but one woman since I have been here, and should not have been by her if she could have avoided it. I 've never been to church yet, and probably shall not be soon. I stay away because I am conscious I should not know how to behave myself.

I am often thinking of what we said about your coming to live at Springfield. I am afraid you would not be satisfied. There is a great deal of flourishing about in carriages here, which it would be your doom to see without sharing it. You would have to be poor, without the means of hiding your poverty. Do you believe you could bear that patiently? Whatever woman may cast her lot with mine, should any ever do so, it is my intention to do all in my power to make her happy and contented; and there is nothing I can imagine that would make me more unhappy than to fail in the effort. I know I should be much happier with you than the way I am, provided I saw no signs of discontent in you. What you have said to me may have been in the way of jest, or I may have misunderstood you. If so, then let it be forgotten; if otherwise, I much wish you would think seriously before you decide. What I have said I will most positively abide by, provided you wish it. My opinion is that you had better not do it. You have not been accustomed to hardship, and it may be more severe than you now imagine. I know you are capable of thinking correctly on any subject, and if you deliberate maturely upon this subject before you decide, then I am willing to abide your decision.

You must write me a good long letter after you get this. You have nothing else to do, and though it might not seem interesting to you after you had written it, it would be a good deal of company to me in this "busy wilderness." Tell your sister I don't want to hear any more about selling out and moving. That gives me the "hypo" whenever I think of it.

Yours, etc., LINCOLN.

TO JOHN BENNETT.
SPRINGFIELD, ILL., Aug. 5, 1837.
JOHN BENNETT, ESQ.

DEAR SIR:-Mr. Edwards tells me you wish to know whether the act to which your own incorporation provision was attached passed into a law. It did. You can organize under the general incorporation law as soon as you choose.

I also tacked a provision onto a fellow's bill to authorize the relocation of the road from Salem down to your town, but I am not certain whether or not the bill passed, neither do I suppose I can ascertain before the law will be published, if it is a law. Bowling Greene, Bennette Abe? and yourself are appointed to make the change. No news. No excitement except a little about the election of Monday next.

I suppose, of course, our friend Dr. Heney stands no chance in your diggings.

Your friend and humble servant, A. LINCOLN.

TO MARY OWENS.
SPRINGFIELD, Aug. 16, 1837

FRIEND MARY: You will no doubt think it rather strange that I should write you a letter on the same day on which we parted, and I can only account for it by supposing that seeing you lately makes me think of you more than usual; while at our late meeting we had but few expressions of thoughts. You must know that I cannot see you, or think of you, with entire indifference; and yet it may be that you are mistaken in regard to what my real feelings toward you are.

If I knew you were not, I should not have troubled you with this letter. Perhaps any other man would know enough without information; but I consider it my peculiar right to plead ignorance, and your bounden duty to allow the plea.

I want in all cases to do right; and most particularly so in all cases with women.

I want, at this particular time, more than any thing else to do right with you; and if I knew it would be doing right, as I rather suspect it would, to let you alone I would do it. And, for the purpose of making the matter as plain as possible, I now say that you can drop the subject, dismiss your thoughts (if you ever had any) from me for ever and leave this letter unanswered without calling forth one accusing murmur from me. And I will even go further and say that, if it will add anything to your comfort or peace of mind to do so, it is my sincere wish that you should. Do not understand by this that I wish to cut your acquaintance. I mean no such thing. What I do wish is that our further acquaintance shall depend upon yourself. If such further acquaintance would contribute nothing to your happiness, I am sure it would not to mine. If you feel yourself in any degree bound to me, I am now willing to release you, provided you wish it; while on the other hand I am willing and even anxious to bind you faster if I can be convinced that it will, in any considerable degree, add to your happiness. This, indeed, is the whole question with me. Nothing would make me more miserable than to believe you miserable, nothing more happy than to know you were so.

In what I have now said, I think I cannot be misunderstood; and to make myself understood is the only object of this letter.

If it suits you best not to answer this, farewell. A long life and a merry one attend you. But, if you conclude to write back, speak as plainly as I do. There can neither be harm nor danger in saying to me anything you think, just in the manner you think it. My respects to your sister.

Your friend, LINCOLN.

LEGAL SUIT OF WIDOW
v.s. Gen. ADAMS
TO THE PEOPLE.
"SANGAMON JOURNAL," SPRINGFIELD, ILL., Aug. 19, 1837.

In accordance with our determination, as expressed last week, we present to the reader the articles which were published in hand-bill form, in reference to the case of the heirs of Joseph Anderson vs. James Adams. These articles can now be read uninfluenced by personal or party feeling, and with the sole motive of learning the truth. When that is done, the reader can pass his own judgment on the matters at issue.

We only regret in this case, that the publications were not made some weeks before the election. Such a course might have prevented the expressions of regret, which have often been heard since, from different individuals, on account of the disposition they made of their votes.

To the Public:

It is well known to most of you, that there is existing at this time considerable excitement in regard to Gen. Adams's titles to certain tracts of land, and the manner in which he acquired them. As I understand, the Gen. charges that the whole has been gotten up by a knot of lawyers to injure his election; and as I am one of the knot to which he refers, and as I happen to be in possession of facts connected with the matter, I will, in as brief a manner as possible, make a statement of them, together with the means by which I arrived at the knowledge of them.

Sometime in May or June last, a widow woman, by the name of Anderson, and her son, who resides in Fulton county, came to Springfield, for the purpose as they said of selling a ten acre lot of ground lying near town, which they claimed as the property of the deceased husband and father.

When they reached town they found the land was claimed by Gen. Adams. John T. Stuart and myself were employed to look into the matter, and if it was thought we could do so with any prospect of success, to commence a suit for the land. I went immediately to the recorder's office to examine Adams's title, and found that the land had been entered by one Dixon, deeded by Dixon to Thomas, by Thomas to one Miller, and by Miller to Gen. Adams. The oldest of these three deeds was about ten or eleven years old, and the latest more than five, all recorded at the same time, and that within less than one year. This I thought a suspicious circumstance, and I was thereby induced to examine the deeds very closely, with a view to the discovery of some defect by which to overturn the title, being almost convinced then it was founded in fraud. I discovered that in the deed from Thomas to Miller, although Miller's name stood in a sort of marginal note on the record book, it was nowhere in the deed itself. I told the fact to Talbott, the recorder, and proposed to him that he should go to Gen. Adams's and get the original deed, and compare it with the record, and thereby ascertain whether the defect was in the original or there was merely an error in the recording. As Talbott afterwards told me, he went to the General's, but not finding him at home, got the deed from his son, which, when compared with the record, proved what we had discovered was merely an error of the recorder. After Mr. Talbott corrected the record, he brought the original to our office, as I then thought and think yet, to show us that it was right. When he came into the room he handed the deed to me, remarking that the fault was all his own. On opening it, another paper fell out of it, which on examination proved to be an assignment of a judgment in the Circuit Court of Sangamon County from Joseph Anderson, the late husband of the widow above named, to James Adams, the judgment being in favor of said Anderson against one Joseph Miller. Knowing that this judgment had some connection with the land affair, I immediately took a copy of it, which is word for word, letter for letter and cross for cross as follows:

Joseph Anderson, vs. Joseph Miller.

Judgment in Sangamon Circuit Court against Joseph Miller obtained on a note originally 25 dolls and interest thereon accrued. I assign all my right, title and interest to James Adams which is in consideration of a debt I owe said Adams.

his JOSEPH x ANDERSON. mark.

As the copy shows, it bore date May 10, 1827; although the judgment assigned by it was not obtained until the October afterwards, as may be seen by any one on the records of the Circuit Court. Two other strange circumstances attended it which cannot be represented by a copy. One of them was, that the date "1827" had first been made "1837" and, without the figure "3," being fully obliterated, the figure "2" had afterwards been made on top of it; the other was that, although the date was ten years old, the writing on it, from the freshness of its appearance, was thought by many, and I believe by all who saw it, not to be more than a week old. The paper on which it was written had a very old appearance; and there were some old figures on the back of it which made the freshness of the writing on the face of it much more striking than I suppose it otherwise might have been. The reader's curiosity is no doubt excited to know what connection this assignment had with the land in question. The story is this: Dixon sold and deeded the land to Thomas; Thomas sold it to Anderson; but before he gave a deed, Anderson sold it to Miller, and took Miller's note for the purchase money. When this note became due, Anderson sued Miller on it, and Miller procured an injunction from the Court of Chancery to stay the collection of the money until he should get a deed for the land. Gen. Adams was employed as an attorney by Anderson in this chancery suit, and at the October term, 1827, the injunction was dissolved, and a judgment given in favor of Anderson against Miller; and it was provided that Thomas was to execute a deed for the land in favor of Miller and deliver it to Gen. Adams, to be held up by him till Miller paid the judgment, and then to deliver it to him. Miller left the county without paying the judgment. Anderson moved to Fulton county, where he has since died When the widow came to Springfield last May or June, as before mentioned, and found the land deeded to Gen. Adams by Miller, she was naturally led to inquire why the money due upon the judgment had not been sent to them, inasmuch as he, Gen. Adams, had no authority to deliver Thomas's deed to Miller until the money was paid. Then it was the General told her, or perhaps her son, who came with her, that Anderson, in his lifetime, had assigned the judgment to him, Gen. Adams. I am now told that the General is exhibiting an assignment of the same judgment bearing date "1828" and in other respects differing from the one described; and that he is asserting that no such assignment as the one copied by me ever existed; or if there did, it was forged between Talbott and the lawyers, and slipped into his papers for the purpose of injuring him. Now, I can only say that I know precisely such a one did exist, and that Ben. Talbott, Wm. Butler, C.R. Matheny, John T. Stuart, Judge Logan, Robert Irwin, P. C. Canedy and S. M. Tinsley, all saw and examined it, and that at least one half of them will swear that IT WAS IN GENERAL ADAMS'S HANDWRITING!! And further, I know that Talbott will swear that he got it out of the General's possession, and returned it into his possession again. The assignment which the

106

General is now exhibiting purports to have been by Anderson in writing. The one I copied was signed with a cross.

I am told that Gen. Neale says that he will swear that he heard Gen. Adams tell young Anderson that the assignment made by his father was signed with a cross.

The above are 'facts,' as stated. I leave them without comment. I have given the names of persons who have knowledge of these facts, in order that any one who chooses may call on them and ascertain how far they will corroborate my statements. I have only made these statements because I am known by many to be one of the individuals against whom the charge of forging the assignment and slipping it into the General's papers has been made, and because our silence might be construed into a confession of its truth. I shall not subscribe my name; but I hereby authorize the editor of the Journal to give it up to any one that may call for it.

LINCOLN AND TALBOTT IN REPLY TO GEN. ADAMS. "SANGAMON JOURNAL," SPRINGFIELD, ILL., Oct. 28, 1837.

In the Republican of this morning a publication of Gen. Adams's appears, in which my name is used quite unreservedly. For this I thank the General. I thank him because it gives me an opportunity, without appearing obtrusive, of explaining a part of a former publication of mine, which appears to me to have been misunderstood by many.

In the former publication alluded to, I stated, in substance, that Mr. Talbott got a deed from a son of Gen. Adams's for the purpose of correcting a mistake that had occurred on the record of the said deed in the recorder's office; that he corrected the record, and brought the deed and handed it to me, and that on opening the deed, another paper, being the assignment of a judgment, fell out of it. This statement Gen. Adams and the editor of the Republican have seized upon as a most palpable evidence of fabrication and falsehood. They set themselves gravely about proving that the assignment could not have been in the deed when Talbott got it from young Adams, as he, Talbott, would have seen it when he opened the deed to correct the record. Now, the truth is, Talbott did see the assignment when he opened the deed, or at least he told me he did on the same day; and I only omitted to say so, in my former publication, because it was a matter of such palpable and necessary inference. I had stated that Talbott had corrected the record by the deed; and of course he must have opened it; and, just as the General and his friends argue, must have seen the assignment. I omitted to state the fact of Talbott's seeing the assignment, because its existence was so necessarily connected with other facts which I did state, that I thought the greatest dunce could not but understand it. Did I say Talbott had not seen it? Did I say anything that was inconsistent with his having seen it before? Most certainly I did neither; and if I did not, what becomes of the argument? These logical gentlemen can sustain their argument only by assuming that I did say negatively everything that I did not say affirmatively; and upon the same assumption, we may expect to find the General, if a little harder pressed for argument, saying that I said Talbott came to our office with his head downward, not that I actually said so, but because I omitted to say he came feet downward.

In his publication to-day, the General produces the affidavit of Reuben Radford, in which it is said that Talbott told Radford that he did not find the assignment in the deed, in the recording of which the error was committed, but that he found it wrapped in another paper in the recorder's office, upon which statement the Genl. comments as follows, to wit: "If it be true as stated by Talbott to Radford, that he found the assignment wrapped up in another paper at his office, that contradicts the statement of Lincoln that it fell out of the deed."

Is common sense to be abused with such sophistry? Did I say what Talbott found it in? If Talbott did find it in another paper at his office, is that any reason why he could not have folded it in a deed and brought it to my office? Can any one be so far duped as to be made believe that what may have happened at Talbot's office at one time is inconsistent with what happened at my office at another time?

Now Talbott's statement of the case as he makes it to me is this, that he got a bunch of deeds from young Adams, and that he knows he found the assignment in the bunch, but he is not certain which particular deed it was in, nor is he certain whether it was folded in the same deed out of which it was taken, or another one, when it was brought to my office. Is this a mysterious story? Is there anything suspicious about it?

108

"But it is useless to dwell longer on this point. Any man who is not wilfully blind can see at a flash, that there is no discrepancy, and Lincoln has shown that they are not only inconsistent with truth, but each other"—I can only say, that I have shown that he has done no such thing; and if the reader is disposed to require any other evidence than the General's assertion, he will be of my opinion.

Excepting the General's most flimsy attempt at mystification, in regard to a discrepance between Talbott and myself, he has not denied a single statement that I made in my hand-bill. Every material statement that I made has been sworn to by men who, in former times, were thought as respectable as General Adams. I stated that an assignment of a judgment, a copy of which I gave, had existed—Benj. Talbott, C. R. Matheny, Wm. Butler, and Judge Logan swore to its existence. I stated that it was said to be in Gen. Adams's handwriting—the same men swore it was in his handwriting. I stated that Talbott would swear that he got it out of Gen. Adams's possession—Talbott came forward and did swear it.

Bidding adieu to the former publication, I now propose to examine the General's last gigantic production. I now propose to point out some discrepancies in the General's address; and such, too, as he shall not be able to escape from. Speaking of the famous assignment, the General says: "This last charge, which was their last resort, their dying effort to render my character infamous among my fellow citizens, was manufactured at a certain lawyer's office in the town, printed at the office of the Sangamon Journal, and found its way into the world some time between two days just before the last election." Now turn to Mr. Keys' affidavit, in which you will find the following, viz.: "I certify that some time in May or the early part of June, 1837, I saw at Williams's corner a paper purporting to be an assignment from Joseph Anderson to James Adams, which assignment was signed by a mark to Anderson's name," etc. Now mark, if Keys saw the assignment on the last of May or first of June, Gen. Adams tells a falsehood when he says it was manufactured just before the election, which was on the 7th of August; and if it was manufactured just before the election, Keys tells a falsehood when he says he saw it on the last of May or first of June. Either Keys or the General is irretrievably in for it; and in the General's very condescending language, I say "Let them settle it between them."

Now again, let the reader, bearing in mind that General Adams has unequivocally said, in one part of his address, that the charge in relation to the assignment was manufactured just before the election, turn to the affidavit of Peter S. Weber, where the following will be found viz.: "I, Peter S. Weber, do certify that from the best of my recollection, on the day or day after Gen. Adams started for the Illinois Rapids, in May last, that I was at the house of Gen. Adams, sitting in the kitchen, situated on the back part of the house, it being in the afternoon, and that Benjamin Talbott came around the house, back into the kitchen, and appeared wild and confused, and that he laid a package of papers on the kitchen table and requested that they should be handed to Lucian. He made no apology for coming to the kitchen, nor for not handing them to Lucian himself, but showed the token of being frightened and confused both in demeanor and speech and for what cause I could not apprehend."

Commenting on Weber's affidavit, Gen. Adams asks, "Why this fright and confusion?" I reply that this is a question for the General himself. Weber says that it was in May, and if so, it is most clear that Talbott was not frightened on account of the assignment, unless the General lies when he says the assignment charge was manufactured just before the election. Is it not a strong evidence, that the General is not traveling with the pole-star of truth in his front, to see him in one part of his address roundly asserting that the assignment was manufactured just before the election, and then, forgetting that position, procuring Weber's most foolish affidavit, to prove that Talbott had been engaged in manufacturing it two months before?

In another part of his address, Gen. Adams says: "That I hold an assignment of said judgment, dated the 20th of May, 1828, and signed by said Anderson, I have never pretended to deny or conceal, but stated that fact in one of my circulars previous to the election, and also in answer to a bill in chancery." Now I pronounce this statement unqualifiedly false, and shall not rely on the word or oath of any man to sustain me in what I say; but will let the whole be decided by reference to the circular and answer in chancery of which the General speaks. In his circular he did speak of an assignment; but he did not say it bore date 20th of May, 1828; nor did he say it bore any date. In his answer in chancery, he did say that he had an assignment; but he did not say that it bore date the 20th May, 1828; but so far from it, he said on oath (for he swore to the answer) that as well as recollected, he obtained it in 1827. If any one doubts, let him examine the circular and answer for himself. They are both accessible.

It will readily be observed that the principal part of Adams's defense rests upon the argument that if he had been base enough to forge an assignment he would not have been fool enough to forge one that would not cover the case. This argument he used in his circular before the election. The Republican has used it at least once, since then; and Adams uses it again in his publication of to-day. Now I pledge myself to show that he is just such a fool that he and his friends have contended it was impossible for him to be. Recollect—he says he has a genuine assignment; and that he got Joseph Klein's affidavit, stating that he had seen it, and that he believed the signature to have been executed by the same hand that signed Anderson's name to the answer in chancery. Luckily Klein took a copy of this genuine assignment, which I have been permitted to see; and hence I know it does not cover the case. In the first place it is headed "Joseph Anderson vs. Joseph Miller," and heads off "Judgment in Sangamon Circuit Court." Now, mark, there never was a case in Sangamon Circuit Court entitled Joseph Anderson vs. Joseph Miller. The case mentioned in my former publication, and the only one between these parties that ever existed in the Circuit Court, was entitled Joseph Miller vs. Joseph Anderson, Miller being the plaintiff. What then becomes of all their sophistry about Adams not being fool enough to forge an assignment that would not cover the case? It is certain that the present one does not cover the case; and if he got it honestly, it is still clear that he was fool enough to pay for an assignment that does not cover the case.

The General asks for the proof of disinterested witnesses. Whom does he consider disinterested? None can be more so than those who have already testified against him. No one of them had the least interest on earth, so far as I can learn, to injure him. True, he says they had conspired against him; but if the testimony of an angel from Heaven were introduced against him, he would make the same charge of conspiracy. And now I put the question to every reflecting man, Do you believe that Benjamin Talbott, Chas. R. Matheny, William Butler and Stephen T. Logan, all sustaining high and spotless characters, and justly proud of them, would deliberately perjure themselves, without any motive whatever, except to injure a man's election; and that, too, a man who had been a candidate, time out of mind, and yet who had never been elected to any office?

Adams's assurance, in demanding disinterested testimony, is surpassing. He brings in the affidavit of his own son, and even of Peter

111

S. Weber, with whom I am not acquainted, but who, I suppose, is some black or mulatto boy, from his being kept in the kitchen, to prove his points; but when such a man as Talbott, a man who, but two years ago, ran against Gen. Adams for the office of Recorder and beat him more than four votes to one, is introduced against him, he asks the community, with all the consequence of a lord, to reject his testimony.

I might easily write a volume, pointing out inconsistencies between the statements in Adams's last address with one another, and with other known facts; but I am aware the reader must already be tired with the length of this article. His opening statements, that he was first accused of being a Tory, and that he refuted that; that then the Sampson's ghost story was got up, and he refuted that; that as a last resort, a dying effort, the assignment charge was got up is all as false as hell, as all this community must know. Sampson's ghost first made its appearance in print, and that, too, after Keys swears he saw the assignment, as any one may see by reference to the files of papers; and Gen. Adams himself, in reply to the Sampson's ghost story, was the first man that raised the cry of toryism, and it was only by way of set-off, and never in seriousness, that it was bandied back at him. His effort is to make the impression that his enemies first made the charge of toryism and he drove them from that, then Sampson's ghost, he drove them from that, then finally the assignment charge was manufactured just before election. Now, the only general reply he ever made to the Sampson's ghost and tory charges he made at one and the same time, and not in succession as he states; and the date of that reply will show, that it was made at least a month after the date on which Keys swears he saw the Anderson assignment. But enough. In conclusion I will only say that I have a character to defend as well as Gen. Adams, but I disdain to whine about it as he does. It is true I have no children nor kitchen boys; and if I had, I should scorn to lug them in to make affidavits for me.

A. LINCOLN, September 6, 1837.

Gen. ADAMS CONTROVERSY— CONTINUED TO THE PUBLIC.

"SANGAMON JOURNAL," Springfield, Ill, Oct.28, 1837.

Such is the turn which things have taken lately, that when Gen. Adams writes a book, I am expected to write a commentary on it. In the Republican of this morning he has presented the world with a new work of six columns in length; in consequence of which I must beg the room of one column in the Journal. It is obvious that a minute reply cannot be made in one column to everything that can be said in six; and, consequently, I hope that expectation will be answered if I reply to such parts of the General's publication as are worth replying to.

It may not be improper to remind the reader that in his publication of Sept. 6th General Adams said that the assignment charge was manufactured just before the election; and that in reply I proved that statement to be false by Keys, his own witness. Now, without attempting to explain, he furnishes me with another witness (Tinsley) by which the same thing is proved, to wit, that the assignment was not manufactured just before the election; but that it was some weeks before. Let it be borne in mind that Adams made this statement—has himself furnished two witnesses to prove its falsehood, and does not attempt to deny or explain it. Before going farther, let a pin be stuck here, labeled "One lie proved and confessed." On the 6th of September he said he had before stated in the hand-bill that he held an assignment dated May 20th, 1828, which in reply I pronounced to be false, and referred to the hand-bill for the truth of what I said. This week he forgets to make any explanation of this. Let another pin be stuck here, labelled as before. I mention these things because, if, when I convict him in one falsehood, he is permitted to shift his ground and pass it by in silence, there can be no end to this controversy.

The first thing that attracts my attention in the General's present production is the information he is pleased to give to "those who are made to suffer at his (my) hands."

Under present circumstances, this cannot apply to me, for I am not a widow nor an orphan: nor have I a wife or children who might by possibility become such. Such, however, I have no doubt, have been, and will again be made to suffer at his hands! Hands! Yes, they are the mischievous agents. The next thing I shall notice is his favorite expression, "not of lawyers, doctors and others," which he is so fond of applying to all who dare expose his rascality. Now, let it be remembered that when he first came to this country he attempted to impose himself upon the community as a lawyer, and actually carried the attempt so far as to induce a man who was under a charge of murder to entrust the defence of his life in his hands, and finally took his money and got him hanged. Is this the man that is to raise a breeze in his favor by abusing lawyers? If he is not himself a lawyer, it is for the lack of sense, and not of inclination. If he is not a lawyer, he is a liar, for he proclaimed himself a lawyer, and got a man hanged by depending on him.

Passing over such parts of the article as have neither fact nor argument in them, I come to the question asked by Adams whether any person ever saw the assignment in his possession. This is an insult to common sense. Talbott has sworn once and repeated time and again, that he got it out of Adams's possession and returned it into the same possession. Still, as though he was addressing fools, he has assurance to ask if any person ever saw it in his possession.

Next I quote a sentence, "Now my son Lucian swears that when Talbott called for the deed, that he, Talbott, opened it and pointed out the error." True. His son Lucian did swear as he says; and in doing so, he swore what I will prove by his own affidavit to be a falsehood. Turn to Lucian's affidavit, and you will there see that Talbott called for the deed by which to correct an error on the record. Thus it appears that the error in question was on the record, and not in the deed. How then could Talbott open the deed and point out the error? Where a thing is not, it cannot be pointed out. The error was not in the deed, and of course could not be pointed out there. This does not merely prove that the error could not be pointed out, as Lucian swore it was; but it proves, too, that the deed was not opened in his presence with a special view to the error, for if it had been, he could not have failed to see that there was no error in it. It is easy enough to see why Lucian swore this. His object was to prove that the assignment was not in the deed when Talbott got it: but it was discovered he could not swear this safely, without first swearing the deed was opened—and if he swore it was opened, he must show a motive for opening it, and the conclusion with him and his father was that the pointing out the error would appear the most plausible.

For the purpose of showing that the assignment was not in the bundle when Talbott got it, is the story introduced into Lucian's affidavit that the deeds were counted. It is a remarkable fact, and one that should stand as a warning to all liars and fabricators, that in this short affidavit of Lucian's he only attempted to depart from the truth, so far as I have the means of knowing, in two points, to wit, in the opening the deed and pointing out the error and the counting of the deeds,—and in both of these he caught himself. About the counting, he caught himself thus—after saying the bundle contained five deeds and a lease, he proceeds, "and I saw no other papers than the said deed and lease." First he has six papers, and then he saw none but two; for "my son Lucian's" benefit, let a pin be stuck here.

Adams again adduces the argument, that he could not have forged the assignment, for the reason that he could have had no motive for it. With those that know the facts there is no absence of motive. Admitting the paper which he has filed in the suit to be genuine, it is clear that it cannot answer the purpose for which he designs it. Hence his motive for making one that he supposed would answer is obvious. His making the date too old is also easily enough accounted for. The records were not in his hands, and then, there being some considerable talk upon this particular subject, he knew he could not examine the records to ascertain the precise dates without subjecting himself to suspicion; and hence he concluded to try it by guess, and, as it turned out, missed it a little. About Miller's deposition I have a word to say. In the first place, Miller's answer to the first question shows upon its face that he had been tampered with, and the answer dictated to him. He was asked if he knew Joel Wright and James Adams; and above three-fourths of his answer consists of what he knew about Joseph Anderson, a man about whom nothing had been asked, nor a word said in the question—a fact that can only be accounted for upon the supposition that Adams had secretly told him what he wished him to swear to.

Another of Miller's answers I will prove both by common sense and the Court of Record is untrue. To one question he answers, "Anderson brought a suit against me before James Adams, then an acting justice of the peace in Sangamon County, before whom he obtained a judgment.

"Q.—Did you remove the same by injunction to the Sangamon Circuit Court? Ans.—I did remove it."

Now mark—it is said he removed it by injunction. The word "injunction" in common language imports a command that some person or thing shall not move or be removed; in law it has the same meaning. An injunction issuing out of chancery to a justice of the peace is a command to him to stop all proceedings in a named case until further orders. It is not an order to remove but to stop or stay something that is already moving. Besides this, the records of the Sangamon Circuit Court show that the judgment of which Miller swore was never removed into said Court by injunction or otherwise.

I have now to take notice of a part of Adams's address which in the order of time should have been noticed before. It is in these words: "I

115

have now shown, in the opinion of two competent judges, that the handwriting of the forged assignment differed from mine, and by one of them that it could not be mistaken for mine." That is false. Tinsley no doubt is the judge referred to; and by reference to his certificate it will be seen that he did not say the handwriting of the assignment could not be mistaken for Adams's—nor did he use any other expression substantially, or anything near substantially, the same. But if Tinsley had said the handwriting could not be mistaken for Adams's, it would have been equally unfortunate for Adams: for it then would have contradicted Keys, who says, "I looked at the writing and judged it the said Adams's or a good imitation."

Adams speaks with much apparent confidence of his success on attending lawsuits, and the ultimate maintenance of his title to the land in question. Without wishing to disturb the pleasure of his dream, I would say to him that it is not impossible that he may yet be taught to sing a different song in relation to the matter.

At the end of Miller's deposition, Adams asks, "Will Mr. Lincoln now say that he is almost convinced my title to this ten acre tract of land is founded in fraud?" I answer, I will not. I will now change the phraseology so as to make it run—I am quite convinced, &c. I cannot pass in silence Adams's assertion that he has proved that the forged assignment was not in the deed when it came from his house by Talbott, the recorder. In this, although Talbott has sworn that the assignment was in the bundle of deeds when it came from his house, Adams has the unaccountable assurance to say that he has proved the contrary by Talbott. Let him or his friends attempt to show wherein he proved any such thing by Talbott.

In his publication of the 6th of September he hinted to Talbott, that he might be mistaken. In his present, speaking of Talbott and me he says "They may have been imposed upon." Can any man of the least penetration fail to see the object of this? After he has stormed and raged till he hopes and imagines he has got us a little scared he wishes to softly whisper in our ears, "If you'll quit I will." If he could get us to say that some unknown, undefined being had slipped the assignment into our hands without our knowledge, not a doubt remains but that he would immediately discover that we were the purest men on earth. This is the ground he evidently wishes us to understand he is willing to compromise upon. But we ask no such charity at his hands. We are neither mistaken nor imposed upon. We have made the statements we have because we know them to be true and we choose to live or die by them.

Esq. Carter, who is Adams's friend, personal and political, will recollect, that, on the 5th of this month, he (Adams), with a great affectation of modesty, declared that he would never introduce his own child as a witness. Notwithstanding this affectation of modesty, he has in his present publication introduced his child as witness; and as if to show with how much contempt he could treat his own declaration, he has had this same Esq. Carter to administer the oath to him. And so important a witness does he consider him, and so entirely does the whole of his entire present production depend upon the testimony of his child, that in it he has mentioned "my son," "my son Lucian," "Lucian, my son," and the like expressions no less than fifteen different times. Let it be remembered here, that I have shown the affidavit of "my darling son Lucian" to be false by the evidence apparent on its own face; and I now ask if that affidavit be taken away what foundation will the fabric have left to stand upon?

General Adams's publications and out-door maneuvering, taken in connection with the editorial articles of the Republican, are not more foolish and contradictory than they are ludicrous and amusing. One week the Republican notifies the public that Gen. Adams is preparing an instrument that will tear, rend, split, rive, blow up, confound, overwhelm, annihilate, extinguish, exterminate, burst asunder, and grind to powder all its slanderers, and particularly Talbott and Lincoln—all of which is to be done in due time.

Then for two or three weeks all is calm—not a word said. Again the Republican comes forth with a mere passing remark that "public" opinion has decided in favor of Gen. Adams, and intimates that he will give himself no more trouble about the matter. In the meantime Adams himself is prowling about and, as Burns says of the devil, "For prey, and holes and corners tryin'," and in one instance goes so far as to take an old acquaintance of mine several steps from a crowd and, apparently weighed down with the importance of his business, gravely and solemnly asks him if "he ever heard Lincoln say he was a deist."

Anon the Republican comes again. "We invite the attention of the public to General Adams's communication," &c. "The victory is a great one, the triumph is overwhelming." I really believe the editor of the Illinois Republican is fool enough to think General Adams leads off—"Authors most egregiously mistaken &c. Most woefully shall their presumption be punished," &c. (Lord have mercy on us.) "The

117

hour is yet to come, yea, nigh at hand—(how long first do you reckon?)—when the Journal and its junto shall say, I have appeared too early." "Their infamy shall be laid bare to the public gaze." Suddenly the General appears to relent at the severity with which he is treating us and he exclaims: "The condemnation of my enemies is the inevitable result of my own defense." For your health's sake, dear Gen., do not permit your tenderness of heart to afflict you so much on our account. For some reason (perhaps because we are killed so quickly) we shall never be sensible of our suffering.

Farewell, General. I will see you again at court if not before— when and where we will settle the question whether you or the widow shall have the land.

A. LINCOLN. October 18, 1837.

1838

TO Mrs. O. H. BROWNING—A FARCE
SPRINGFIELD, April 1, 1838.

DEAR MADAM:—Without apologizing for being egotistical, I shall make the history of so much of my life as has elapsed since I saw you the subject of this letter. And, by the way, I now discover that, in order to give a full and intelligible account of the things I have done and suffered since I saw you, I shall necessarily have to relate some that happened before.

It was, then, in the autumn of 1836 that a married lady of my acquaintance, and who was a great friend of mine, being about to pay a visit to her father and other relatives residing in Kentucky, proposed to me that on her return she would bring a sister of hers with her on condition that I would engage to become her brother-in-law with all convenient despatch. I, of course, accepted the proposal, for you know I could not have done otherwise had I really been averse to it; but privately, between you and me, I was most confoundedly well pleased with the project. I had seen the said sister some three years before, thought her intelligent and agreeable, and saw no good objection to plodding life through hand in hand with her. Time passed on; the lady took her journey and in due time returned, sister in company, sure enough. This astonished me a little, for it appeared to me that her coming so readily showed that she was a trifle too willing, but on reflection it occurred to me that she might have been prevailed on by her married sister to come without anything concerning me ever having been mentioned to her, and so I concluded that if no other objection presented itself, I would consent to waive this. All this occurred to me on hearing of her arrival in the neighborhood—for, be it remembered, I had not yet seen her, except about three years previous, as above mentioned. In a few days we had an interview, and, although I had seen her before, she did not look as my imagination had pictured her. I knew she was over-size, but she now appeared a fair match for Falstaff. I knew she was called an "old maid," and I felt no doubt of the truth of at least half of the appellation, but now, when I beheld her, I could not for my life avoid thinking of my mother; and this, not from withered features,—for her skin was too full of fat to permit of its contracting into wrinkles,—but from her want of teeth, weather-beaten appearance in general, and from a kind of notion that ran in my head that nothing could have commenced at the size of infancy and reached her present bulk in less than thirty-five or forty years; and in short, I was not at all pleased with her. But what could I do? I had told her sister that I would take her for better or for worse, and I made a point of honor and conscience in all things to stick to my word especially if others had been induced to act on it which in this case I had no doubt they had, for I was now fairly convinced that no other man on earth would have her, and hence the conclusion that they were bent on holding me to my bargain.

"Well," thought I, "I have said it, and, be the consequences what they may, it shall not be my fault if I fail to do it." At once I determined to consider her my wife; and, this done, all my powers of discovery were put to work in search of perfections in her which might be fairly set off against her defects. I tried to imagine her handsome, which, but for her unfortunate corpulency, was actually true. Exclusive of this no woman that I have ever seen has a finer face. I also tried to convince myself that the mind was much more to be valued than the person; and in this she was not inferior, as I could discover, to any with whom I had been acquainted.

Shortly after this, without coming to any positive understanding with her, I set out for Vandalia, when and where you first saw me. During my stay there I had letters from her which did not change my opinion of either her intellect or intention, but on the contrary confirmed it in both.

All this while, although I was fixed, "firm as the surge-repelling rock," in my resolution, I found I was continually repenting the rashness which had led me to make it. Through life, I have been in no bondage, either real or imaginary, from the thraldom of which I so much desired to be free. After my return home, I saw nothing to change my opinions of her in any particular. She was the same, and so was I. I now spent my time in planning how I might get along through life after my contemplated change of circumstances should have taken place, and how I might procrastinate the evil day for a time, which I really dreaded as much, perhaps more, than an Irishman does the halter.

After all my suffering upon this deeply interesting subject, here I am, wholly, unexpectedly, completely, out of the "scrape"; and now I want to know if you can guess how I got out of it——out, clear, in every sense of the term; no violation of word, honor, or conscience. I don't believe you can guess, and so I might as well tell you at once. As the lawyer says, it was done in the manner following, to wit: After I had delayed the matter as long as I thought I could in honor do (which, by the way, had brought me round into the last fall), I concluded I might as well bring it to a consummation without further delay; and so I mustered my resolution, and made the proposal to her direct; but, shocking to relate, she answered, No. At first I supposed she did it through an affectation of modesty, which I thought but ill became her under the peculiar circumstances of her case; but on my renewal of the charge, I found she repelled it with greater firmness than before. I tried it again and again but with the same success, or rather with the same want of success.

I finally was forced to give it up; at which I very unexpectedly found myself mortified almost beyond endurance. I was mortified, it seemed to me, in a hundred different ways. My vanity was deeply wounded by the reflection that I had been too stupid to discover her intentions, and at the same time never doubting that I understood them perfectly, and also that she, whom I had taught myself to believe nobody else would have, had actually rejected me with all my fancied greatness. And, to cap the whole, I then for the first time began to suspect that I was really a little in love with her. But let it all go. I'll try and outlive it. Others have been made fools of by the girls, but this can never with truth be said of me. I most emphatically in this instance, made a fool of myself. I have now come to the conclusion never again to think of marrying, and for this reason: I can never be satisfied with any one who would be blockhead enough to have me.

When you receive this, write me a long yarn about something to amuse me. Give my respects to Mr. Browning.

Your sincere friend, A. LINCOLN.

1839

REMARKS ON SALE OF PUBLIC LANDS IN THE HOUSE OF REPRESENTATIVES, January 17, 1839.

Mr. Lincoln, from Committee on Finance, to which the subject was referred, made a report on the subject of purchasing of the United States all the unsold lands lying within the limits of the State of Illinois, accompanied by resolutions that this State propose to purchase all unsold lands at twenty-five cents per acre, and pledging the faith of the State to carry the proposal into effect if the government accept the same within two years.

Mr. Lincoln thought the resolutions ought to be seriously considered. In reply to the gentleman from Adams, he said that it was not to enrich the State. The price of the lands may be raised, it was thought by some; by others, that it would be reduced. The conclusion in his mind was that the representatives in this Legislature from the country in which the lands lie would be opposed to raising the price, because it would operate against the settlement of the lands. He referred to the lands in the military tract. They had fallen into the hands of large speculators in consequence of the low price. He was opposed to a low price of land. He thought it was adverse to the interests of the poor settler, because speculators buy them up. He was opposed to a reduction of the price of public lands.

Mr. Lincoln referred to some official documents emanating from Indiana, and compared the progressive population of the two States. Illinois had gained upon that State under the public land system as it is. His conclusion was that ten years from this time Illinois would have no more public land unsold than Indiana now has. He referred also to Ohio. That State had sold nearly all her public lands. She was but twenty years ahead of us, and as our lands were equally salable—more so, as he maintained—we should have no more twenty years from now than she has at present.

Mr. Lincoln referred to the canal lands, and supposed that the policy of the State would be different in regard to them, if the representatives from that section of country could themselves choose the policy; but the representatives from other parts of the State had a veto upon it, and regulated the policy. He thought that if the State had all the lands, the policy of the Legislature would be more liberal to all sections.

He referred to the policy of the General Government. He thought that if the national debt had not been paid, the expenses of the government would not have doubled, as they had done since that debt was paid.

TO —— ROW.
SPRINGFIELD, June 11, 1839

DEAR ROW:

Mr. Redman informs me that you wish me to write you the particulars of a conversation between Dr. Felix and myself relative to you. The Dr. overtook me between Rushville and Beardstown.

He, after learning that I had lived at Springfield, asked if I was acquainted with you. I told him I was. He said you had lately been elected constable in Adams, but that you never would be again. I asked him why. He said the people there had found out that you had been sheriff or deputy sheriff in Sangamon County, and that you came off and left your securities to suffer. He then asked me if I did not know such to be the fact. I told him I did not think you had ever been sheriff or deputy sheriff in Sangamon, but that I thought you had been constable. I further told him that if you had left your securities to suffer in that or any other case, I had never heard of it, and that if it had been so, I thought I would have heard of it.

If the Dr. is telling that I told him anything against you whatever, I authorize you to contradict it flatly. We have no news here.

Your friend, as ever, A. LINCOLN.

SPEECH ON NATIONAL BANK IN THE HALL OF THE HOUSE OF REPRESENTATIVES

SPRINGFIELD, ILLINOIS, December 20, 1839.

FELLOW-CITIZENS:—It is peculiarly embarrassing to me to attempt a continuance of the discussion, on this evening, which has been conducted in this hall on several preceding ones. It is so because on each of those evenings there was a much fuller attendance than now, without any reason for its being so, except the greater interest the community feel in the speakers who addressed them then than they do in him who is to do so now. I am, indeed, apprehensive that the few who have attended have done so more to spare me mortification than in the hope of being interested in anything I may be able to say. This circumstance casts a damp upon my spirits, which I am sure I shall be unable to overcome during the evening. But enough of preface.

The subject heretofore and now to be discussed is the subtreasury scheme of the present administration, as a means of collecting, safe-keeping, transferring, and disbursing, the revenues of the nation, as contrasted with a national bank for the same purposes. Mr. Douglas has said that we (the Whigs) have not dared to meet them (the Locos) in argument on this question. I protest against this assertion. I assert that we have again and again, during this discussion, urged facts and arguments against the subtreasury which they have neither dared to deny nor attempted to answer. But lest some may be led to believe that we really wish to avoid the question, I now propose, in my humble way, to urge those arguments again; at the same time begging the audience to mark well the positions I shall take and the proof I shall offer to sustain them, and that they will not again permit Mr. Douglas or his friends to escape the force of them by a round and groundless assertion that we "dare not meet them in argument."

Of the subtreasury, then, as contrasted with a national bank for the before-enumerated purposes, I lay down the following propositions, to wit: (1) It will injuriously affect the community by its operation on the circulating medium. (2) It will be a more expensive fiscal agent. (3) It will be a less secure depository of the public money. To show the truth of the first proposition, let us take a short review of our condition under the operation of a national bank. It was the depository of the public revenues. Between the collection of those revenues and the disbursement of them by the government, the bank was permitted to and did actually loan them out to individuals, and hence the large amount of money actually collected for revenue purposes, which by any other plan would have been idle a great portion of the time, was kept almost constantly in circulation. Any person who will reflect that money is only valuable while in circulation will readily perceive that any device which will keep the government revenues in constant circulation, instead of being locked up in idleness, is no inconsiderable advantage. By the subtreasury the revenue is to be collected and kept in iron boxes until the government wants it for disbursement; thus robbing the people of the use of it, while the government does not itself need it, and while the money is performing no nobler office than that of rusting in iron boxes. The natural effect of this change of policy, every one will see, is to reduce the quantity of money in circulation. But, again, by the subtreasury scheme the revenue is to be collected in specie. I anticipate that this will be disputed. I expect to hear it said that it is not the policy of the administration to collect the revenue in specie. If it shall, I reply that Mr. Van Buren, in his message recommending the subtreasury, expended nearly a column of that document in an attempt to persuade Congress to provide for the collection of the revenue in specie exclusively; and he concludes with these words:

"It may be safely assumed that no motive of convenience to the citizens requires the reception of bank paper." In addition to this, Mr. Silas Wright, Senator from New York, and the political, personal and confidential friend of Mr. Van Buren, drafted and introduced into the Senate the first subtreasury bill, and that bill provided for ultimately collecting the revenue in specie. It is true, I know, that that clause was stricken from the bill, but it was done by the votes of the Whigs, aided by a portion only of the Van Buren senators. No subtreasury bill has yet become a law, though two or three have been considered by Congress, some with and some without the specie clause; so that I admit there is room for quibbling upon the question of whether the administration favor the exclusive specie doctrine or not; but I take it that the fact that the President at first urged the specie doctrine, and that under his recommendation the first bill introduced embraced it, warrants us in charging it as the policy of the party until their head as publicly recants it as he at first espoused it. I repeat, then, that by the subtreasury the revenue is to be collected in specie. Now mark what the effect of this must be. By all estimates ever made there are but between sixty and eighty millions of specie in the United States. The expenditures of the Government for the year 1838—the last for which we have had the report—were forty millions. Thus it is seen that if the whole revenue be collected in specie, it will take more than half of all the specie in the nation to do it. By this means more than half of all the specie belonging to the fifteen millions of souls who compose the whole population of the country is thrown into the hands of the public office-holders, and other public creditors comprising in number perhaps not more than one quarter of a million, leaving the other fourteen millions and three quarters to get along as they best can, with less than one half of the specie of the country, and whatever rags and shinplasters they may be able to put, and keep, in circulation. By this means, every office-holder and other public creditor may, and most likely will, set up shaver; and a most glorious harvest will the specie-men have of it,—each specie-man, upon a fair division, having to his share the fleecing of about fifty-nine rag-men. In all candor let me ask, was such a system for benefiting the few at the expense of the many ever before devised? And was the sacred name of Democracy ever before made to indorse such an enormity against the rights of the people?

I have already said that the subtreasury will reduce the quantity of money in circulation. This position is strengthened by the recollection that the revenue is to be collected in Specie, so that the mere amount of revenue is not all that is withdrawn, but the amount of paper circulation that the forty millions would serve as a basis to is withdrawn, which would be in a sound state at least one hundred millions. When one hundred millions, or more, of the circulation we now have shall be withdrawn, who can contemplate without terror the distress, ruin, bankruptcy, and beggary that must follow? The man who has purchased any article—say a horse—on credit, at one hundred dollars, when there are two hundred millions circulating in the country, if the quantity be reduced to one hundred millions by the arrival of pay-day, will find the horse but sufficient to pay half the debt; and the other half must either be paid out of his other means, and thereby become a clear loss to him, or go unpaid, and thereby become a clear loss to his creditor. What I have here said of a single case of the purchase of a horse will hold good in every case of a debt existing at the time a reduction in the quantity of money occurs, by whomsoever, and for whatsoever, it may have been contracted. It may be said that what the debtor loses the creditor gains by this operation; but on

125

examination this will be found true only to a very limited extent. It is more generally true that all lose by it—the creditor by losing more of his debts than he gains by the increased value of those he collects; the debtor by either parting with more of his property to pay his debts than he received in contracting them, or by entirely breaking up his business, and thereby being thrown upon the world in idleness.

The general distress thus created will, to be sure, be temporary, because, whatever change may occur in the quantity of money in any community, time will adjust the derangement produced; but while that adjustment is progressing, all suffer more or less, and very many lose everything that renders life desirable. Why, then, shall we suffer a severe difficulty, even though it be but temporary, unless we receive some equivalent for it?

What I have been saying as to the effect produced by a reduction of the quantity of money relates to the whole country. I now propose to show that it would produce a peculiar and permanent hardship upon the citizens of those States and Territories in which the public lands lie. The land-offices in those States and Territories, as all know, form the great gulf by which all, or nearly all, the money in them is swallowed up. When the quantity of money shall be reduced, and consequently everything under individual control brought down in proportion, the price of those lands, being fixed by law, will remain as now. Of necessity it will follow that the produce or labor that now raises money sufficient to purchase eighty acres will then raise but sufficient to purchase forty, or perhaps not that much; and this difficulty and hardship will last as long, in some degree, as any portion of these lands shall remain undisposed of. Knowing, as I well do, the difficulty that poor people now encounter in procuring homes, I hesitate not to say that when the price of the public lands shall be doubled or trebled, or, which is the same thing, produce and labor cut down to one half or one third of their present prices, it will be little less than impossible for them to procure those homes at all....

Well, then, what did become of him? (Postmaster General Barry) Why, the President immediately expressed his high disapprobation of his almost unequaled incapacity and corruption by appointing him to a foreign mission, with a salary and outfit of $18,000 a year! The party now attempt to throw Barry off, and to avoid the responsibility of his sins. Did not the President indorse those sins when, on the very heel of their commission, he appointed their author to the very highest and most honorable office in his gift, and which is but a single step behind the very goal of American political ambition?

I return to another of Mr. Douglas's excuses for the expenditures of 1838, at the same time announcing the pleasing intelligence that this is the last one. He says that ten millions of that year's expenditure was a contingent appropriation, to prosecute an anticipated war with Great Britain on the Maine boundary question. Few words will settle this. First, that the ten millions appropriated was not made till 1839, and consequently could not have been expended in 1838; second, although it was appropriated, it has never been expended at all. Those who heard Mr. Douglas recollect that he indulged himself in a contemptuous expression of pity for me. "Now he's got me," thought I. But when he went on to say that five millions of the expenditure of 1838 were payments of the French indemnities, which I knew to be untrue; that five millions had been for the post-office, which I knew to be untrue; that ten millions had been for the Maine boundary war, which I not only knew to be untrue, but supremely ridiculous also; and when I saw that he was stupid enough to hope that I would permit such groundless and audacious assertions to go unexposed,—I readily consented that, on the score both of veracity and sagacity, the audience should judge whether he or I were the more deserving of the world's contempt.

Mr. Lamborn insists that the difference between the Van Buren party and the Whigs is that, although the former sometimes err in practice, they are always correct in principle, whereas the latter are wrong in principle; and, better to impress this proposition, he uses a figurative expression in these words: "The Democrats are vulnerable in the heel, but they are sound in the head and the heart." The first branch of the figure—that is, that the Democrats are vulnerable in the heel—I admit is not merely figuratively, but literally true. Who that looks but for a moment at their Swartwouts, their Prices, their Harringtons, and their hundreds of others, scampering away with the public money to Texas, to Europe, and to every spot of the earth where a villain may hope to find refuge from justice, can at all doubt that they are most distressingly affected in their heels with a species of "running itch"? It seems that this malady of their heels operates on these sound-headed and honest-hearted creatures very much like the cork leg in the comic song did on its owner: which, when he had once got started on it, the more he tried to stop it, the more it would run away. At the hazard of wearing this point threadbare, I will relate an anecdote which seems too strikingly in point to be omitted. A witty Irish soldier, who was always boasting of his bravery when no danger was near, but who invariably retreated without orders at the first charge of an engagement, being asked by his captain why he did so, replied: "Captain, I have as brave a heart as Julius Caesar ever had; but, somehow or other, whenever danger approaches, my cowardly legs will run away with it." So with Mr. Lamborn's party. They take the public money into their hand for the most laudable purpose that wise heads and honest hearts can dictate; but before they can possibly get it out again, their rascally "vulnerable heels" will run away with them.

Seriously this proposition of Mr. Lamborn is nothing more or less than a request that his party may be tried by their professions instead of their practices. Perhaps no position that the party assumes is more liable to or more deserving of exposure than this very modest request; and nothing but the unwarrantable length to which I have already extended these remarks forbids me now attempting to expose it. For the reason given, I pass it by.

I shall advert to but one more point. Mr. Lamborn refers to the late elections in the States, and from their results confidently predicts that every State in the Union will vote for Mr. Van Buren at the next Presidential election. Address that argument to cowards and to knaves; with the free and the brave it will effect nothing. It may be true; if it must, let it. Many free countries have lost their liberty, and ours may lose hers; but if she shall, be it my proudest plume, not that I was the last to desert, but that I never deserted her. I know that the great volcano at Washington, aroused and directed by the evil spirit that reigns there, is belching forth the lava of political corruption in a current broad and deep, which is sweeping with frightful velocity over the whole length and breadth of the land, bidding fair to leave unscathed no green spot or living thing; while on its bosom are riding, like demons on the waves of hell, the imps of that evil spirit, and fiendishly taunting all those who dare resist its destroying course with the hopelessness of their effort; and, knowing this, I cannot deny that all may be swept away. Broken by it I, too, may be; bow to it I never will. The probability that we may fall in the struggle ought not to deter us from the support of a cause we believe to be just; it shall not deter me. If ever I feel the soul within me elevate and expand to those dimensions not wholly unworthy of its almighty Architect, it is when I contemplate the cause of my country deserted by all the world beside, and I standing up boldly and alone, and hurling defiance at her victorious oppressors. Here, without contemplating consequences, before high heaven and in the face of the world, I swear eternal fidelity to the just cause, as I deem it, of the land of my life, my liberty, and my love. And who that thinks with me will not fearlessly adopt the oath that I take? Let none falter who thinks he is right, and we may succeed. But if, after all, we shall fail, be it so. We still shall have the proud consolation of saying to our consciences, and to the departed shade of our country's freedom, that the cause approved of our judgment, and adored of our hearts, in disaster, in chains, in torture, in death, we never faltered in defending.

TO JOHN T. STUART.
SPRINGFIELD, December 23, 1839.

DEAR STUART:

Dr. Henry will write you all the political news. I write this about some little matters of business. You recollect you told me you had drawn the Chicago Masark money, and sent it to the claimants. A hawk-billed Yankee is here besetting me at every turn I take, saying that Robert Kinzie never received the eighty dollars to which he was entitled. Can you tell me anything about the matter? Again, old Mr. Wright, who lives up South Fork somewhere, is teasing me continually about some deeds which he says he left with you, but which I can find nothing of. Can you tell me where they are? The Legislature is in session and has suffered the bank to forfeit its charter without benefit of clergy. There seems to be little disposition to resuscitate it.

Whenever a letter comes from you to Mrs.＿＿＿＿＿＿ I carry it to her, and then I see Betty; she is a tolerable nice "fellow" now. Maybe I will write again when I get more time.

Your friend as ever, A. LINCOLN

P. S.—The Democratic giant is here, but he is not much worth talking about. A.L.

1840

CIRCULAR FROM WHIG COMMITTEE.
Confidential.

January [1?], 1840.

To MESSRS ———

GENTLEMEN:—In obedience to a resolution of the Whig State convention, we have appointed you the Central Whig Committee of your county. The trust confided to you will be one of watchfulness and labor; but we hope the glory of having contributed to the overthrow of the corrupt powers that now control our beloved country will be a sufficient reward for the time and labor you will devote to it. Our Whig brethren throughout the Union have met in convention, and after due deliberation and mutual concessions have elected candidates for the Presidency and Vice-Presidency not only worthy of our cause, but worthy of the support of every true patriot who would have our country redeemed, and her institutions honestly and faithfully administered. To overthrow the trained bands that are opposed to us whose salaried officers are ever on the watch, and whose misguided followers are ever ready to obey their smallest commands, every Whig must not only know his duty, but must firmly resolve, whatever of time and labor it may cost, boldly and faithfully to do it. Our intention is to organize the whole State, so that every Whig can be brought to the polls in the coming Presidential contest. We cannot do this, however, without your co-operation; and as we do our duty, so we shall expect you to do yours. After due deliberation, the following is the plan of organization, and the duties required of each county committee:

(1) To divide their county into small districts, and to appoint in each a subcommittee, whose duty it shall be to make a perfect list of all the voters in their respective districts, and to ascertain with certainty for whom they will vote. If they meet with men who are doubtful as to the man they will support, such voters should be designated in separate lines, with the name of the man they will probably support.

(2) It will be the duty of said subcommittee to keep a constant watch on the doubtful voters, and from time to time have them talked to by those in whom they have the most confidence, and also to place in their hands such documents as will enlighten and influence them.

(3) It will also be their duty to report to you, at least once a month, the progress they are making, and on election days see that every Whig is brought to the polls.

(4) The subcommittees should be appointed immediately; and by the last of April, at least, they should make their first report.

(5) On the first of each month hereafter we shall expect to hear from you. After the first report of your subcommittees, unless there should be found a great many doubtful voters, you can tell pretty accurately the manner in which your county will vote. In each of your letters to us, you will state the number of certain votes both for and against us, as well as the number of doubtful votes, with your opinion of the manner in which they will be cast.

(6) When we have heard from all the counties, we shall be able to tell with similar accuracy the political complexion of the State. This information will be forwarded to you as soon as received.

(7) Inclosed is a prospectus for a newspaper to be continued until after the Presidential election. It will be superintended by ourselves, and every Whig in the State must take it. It will be published so low that every one can afford it. You must raise a fund and forward us for extra copies,—every county ought to send—fifty or one hundred dollars,—and the copies will be forwarded to you for distribution among our political opponents. The paper will be devoted exclusively to the great cause in which we are engaged. Procure subscriptions, and forward them to us immediately.

(8) Immediately after any election in your county, you must inform us of its results; and as early as possible after any general election we will give you the like information.

(9) A senator in Congress is to be elected by our next Legislature. Let no local interests divide you, but select candidates that can succeed.

(10) Our plan of operations will of course be concealed from every one except our good friends who of right ought to know them.

Trusting much in our good cause, the strength of our candidates, and the determination of the Whigs everywhere to do their duty, we go to the work of organization in this State confident of success. We have the numbers, and if properly organized and exerted, with the gallant

Harrison at our head, we shall meet our foes and conquer them in all parts of the Union.

Address your letters to Dr. A. G. Henry, R. F, Barrett; A. Lincoln, E. D. Baker, J. F. Speed.

TO JOHN T. STUART.
SPRINGFIELD, March 1, 1840
DEAR STUART:

I have never seen the prospects of our party so bright in these parts as they are now. We shall carry this county by a larger majority than we did in 1836, when you ran against May. I do not think my prospects, individually, are very flattering, for I think it probable I shall not be permitted to be a candidate; but the party ticket will succeed triumphantly. Subscriptions to the "Old Soldier" pour in without abatement. This morning I took from the post office a letter from Dubois enclosing the names of sixty subscribers, and on carrying it to Francis I found he had received one hundred and forty more from other quarters by the same day's mail. That is but an average specimen of every day's receipts. Yesterday Douglas, having chosen to consider himself insulted by something in the Journal, undertook to cane Francis in the street. Francis caught him by the hair and jammed him back against a market cart where the matter ended by Francis being pulled away from him. The whole affair was so ludicrous that Francis and everybody else (Douglass excepted) have been laughing about it ever since.

I send you the names of some of the V.B. men who have come out for Harrison about town, and suggest that you send them some documents.

Moses Coffman (he let us appoint him a delegate yesterday), Aaron Coffman, George Gregory, H. M. Briggs, Johnson (at Birchall's Bookstore), Michael Glyn, Armstrong (not Hosea nor Hugh, but a carpenter), Thomas Hunter, Moses Pileher (he was always a Whig and deserves attention), Matthew Crowder Jr., Greenberry Smith; John Fagan, George Fagan, William Fagan (these three fell out with us about Early, and are doubtful now), John M. Cartmel, Noah Rickard, John Rickard, Walter Marsh.

The foregoing should be addressed at Springfield.

Also send some to Solomon Miller and John Auth at Salisbury. Also to Charles Harper, Samuel Harper, and B. C. Harper, and T. J. Scroggins, John Scroggins at Pulaski, Logan County.

Speed says he wrote you what Jo Smith said about you as he passed here. We will procure the names of some of his people here, and send them to you before long. Speed also says you must not fail to send us the New York Journal he wrote for some time since.

Evan Butler is jealous that you never send your compliments to him. You must not neglect him next time.

Your friend, as ever, A. LINCOLN

RESOLUTION IN THE ILLINOIS LEGISLATURE.
November 28, 1840.

In the Illinois House of Representatives, November 28, 1840, Mr. Lincoln offered the following:

Resolved, That so much of the governor's message as relates to fraudulent voting, and other fraudulent practices at elections, be referred to the Committee on Elections, with instructions to said committee to prepare and report to the House a bill for such an act as may in their judgment afford the greatest possible protection of the elective franchise against all frauds of all sorts whatever.

RESOLUTION IN THE ILLINOIS LEGISLATURE.
December 2, 1840.

Resolved, That the Committee on Education be instructed to inquire into the expediency of providing by law for the examination as to the qualification of persons offering themselves as school teachers, that no teacher shall receive any part of the public school fund who shall not have successfully passed such examination, and that they report by bill or otherwise.

REMARKS IN THE ILLINOIS LEGISLATURE.
December 4, 1840

In the House of Representatives, Illinois, December 4, 1840, on presentation of a report respecting petition of H. N. Purple, claiming the seat of Mr. Phelps from Peoria, Mr. Lincoln moved that the House resolve itself into Committee of the Whole on the question, and take it up immediately. Mr. Lincoln considered the question of the highest importance whether an individual had a right to sit in this House or not. The course he should propose would be to take up the evidence and decide upon the facts seriatim.

Mr. Drummond wanted time; they could not decide in the heat of debate, etc.

Mr. Lincoln thought that the question had better be gone into now. In courts of law jurors were required to decide on evidence, without previous study or examination. They were required to know nothing of the subject until the evidence was laid before them for their immediate decision. He thought that the heat of party would be augmented by delay.

The Speaker called Mr. Lincoln to order as being irrelevant; no mention had been made of party heat.

Mr. Drummond said he had only spoken of debate. Mr. Lincoln asked what caused the heat, if it was not party? Mr. Lincoln concluded by urging that the question would be decided now better than hereafter, and he thought with less heat and excitement.

(Further debate, in which Lincoln participated.)

REMARKS IN THE ILLINOIS LEGISLATURE.
December 4, 1840.

In the Illinois House of Representatives, December 4, 1840, House in Committee of the Whole on the bill providing for payment of interest on the State debt,—Mr. Lincoln moved to strike out the body and amendments of the bill, and insert in lieu thereof an amendment which in substance was that the governor be authorized to issue bonds for the payment of the interest; that these be called "interest bonds"; that the taxes accruing on Congress lands as they become taxable be irrevocably set aside and devoted as a fund to the payment of the interest bonds. Mr. Lincoln went into the reasons which appeared to him to render this plan preferable to that of hypothecating the State bonds. By this course we could get along till the next meeting of the Legislature, which was of great importance. To the objection which might be urged that these interest bonds could not be cashed, he replied that if our other bonds could, much more could these, which offered a perfect security, a fund being irrevocably set aside to provide for their redemption. To another objection, that we should be paying compound interest, he would reply that the rapid growth and increase of our resources was in so great a ratio as to outstrip the difficulty; that his object was to do the best that could be done in the present emergency. All agreed that the faith of the State must be preserved; this plan appeared to him preferable to a hypothecation of bonds, which would have to be redeemed and the interest paid. How this was to be done, he could not see; therefore he had, after turning the matter over in every way, devised this measure, which would carry us on till the next Legislature.

(Mr. Lincoln spoke at some length, advocating his measure.)

Lincoln advocated his measure, December 11, 1840.

December 12, 1840, he had thought some permanent provision ought to be made for the bonds to be hypothecated, but was satisfied taxation and revenue could not be connected with it now.

1841

TO JOHN T. STUART—ON DEPRESSION
SPRINGFIELD, Jan 23, 1841

DEAR STUART: I am now the most miserable man living. If what I feel were equally distributed to the whole human family, there would not be one cheerful face on earth. Whether I shall ever be better, I cannot tell; I awfully forbode I shall not. To remain as I am is impossible. I must die or be better, as it appears to me.... I fear I shall be unable to attend any business here, and a change of scene might

135

help me. If I could be myself, I would rather remain at home with Judge Logan. I can write no more.

REMARKS IN THE ILLINOIS LEGISLATURE.
January 23, 1841

In the House of Representatives January 23, 1841, while discussing the continuation of the Illinois and Michigan Canal, Mr. Moore was afraid the holders of the "scrip" would lose.

Mr. Napier thought there was no danger of that; and Mr. Lincoln said he had not examined to see what amount of scrip would probably be needed. The principal point in his mind was this, that nobody was obliged to take these certificates. It is altogether voluntary on their part, and if they apprehend it will fall in their hands they will not take it. Further the loss, if any there be, will fall on the citizens of that section of the country.

This scrip is not going to circulate over an extensive range of country, but will be confined chiefly to the vicinity of the canal. Now, we find the representatives of that section of the country are all in favor of the bill.

When we propose to protect their interests, they say to us: Leave us to take care of ourselves; we are willing to run the risk. And this is reasonable; we must suppose they are competent to protect their own interests, and it is only fair to let them do it.

CIRCULAR FROM WHIG COMMITTEE.
February 9, 1841.
Appeal to the People of the State of Illinois.

FELLOW-CITIZENS:—When the General Assembly, now about adjourning, assembled in November last, from the bankrupt state of the public treasury, the pecuniary embarrassments prevailing in every department of society, the dilapidated state of the public works, and the impending danger of the degradation of the State, you had a right to expect that your representatives would lose no time in devising and adopting measures to avert threatened calamities, alleviate the distresses of the people, and allay the fearful apprehensions in regard to the future prosperity of the State. It was not expected by you that the spirit of party would take the lead in the councils of the State, and make every interest bend to its demands. Nor was it expected that any party would assume to itself the entire control of legislation, and convert the means and offices of the State, and the substance of the people, into aliment for party subsistence. Neither could it have been expected by you that party spirit, however strong its desires and unreasonable its demands, would have passed the sanctuary of the Constitution, and entered with its unhallowed and hideous form into the formation of the judiciary system.

At the early period of the session, measures were adopted by the dominant party to take possession of the State, to fill all public offices with party men, and make every measure affecting the interests of the people and the credit of the State operate in furtherance of their party views. The merits of men and measures therefore became the subject of discussion in caucus, instead of the halls of legislation, and decisions there made by a minority of the Legislature have been executed and carried into effect by the force of party discipline, without any regard whatever to the rights of the people or the interests of the State. The Supreme Court of the State was organized, and judges appointed, according to the provisions of the Constitution, in 1824. The people have never complained of the organization of that court; no attempt has ever before been made to change that department. Respect for public opinion, and regard for the rights and liberties of the people, have hitherto restrained the spirit of party from attacks upon the independence and integrity of the judiciary. The same judges have continued in office since 1824; their decisions have not been the subject of complaint among the people; the integrity and honesty of the court have not been questioned, and it has never been supposed that the court has ever permitted party prejudice or party considerations to operate upon their decisions. The court was made to consist of four judges, and by the Constitution two form a quorum for the transaction of business. With this tribunal, thus constituted, the people have been satisfied for near sixteen years. The same law which organized the Supreme Court in 1824 also established and organized circuit courts to be held in each county in the State, and five circuit judges were appointed to hold those courts. In 1826 the Legislature abolished these circuit courts, repealed the judges out of office, and required the judges of the Supreme Court to hold the circuit courts. The reasons assigned for this change were, first, that the business of the country could be better attended to by the four judges of the Supreme Court than by the two sets of judges; and, second, the state of the public treasury forbade the employment of unnecessary officers. In 1828 a circuit was established north of the Illinois River, in order to meet the wants of the people, and a circuit judge was appointed to hold the courts in that circuit.

In 1834 the circuit-court system was again established throughout the State, circuit judges appointed to hold the courts, and the judges of the Supreme Court were relieved from the performance of circuit court duties. The change was recommended by the then acting governor of the State, General W. L. D. Ewing, in the following terms:

"The augmented population of the State, the multiplied number of organized counties, as well as the increase of business in all, has long since convinced every one conversant with this department of our government of the indispensable necessity of an alteration in our judiciary system, and the subject is therefore recommended to the earnest patriotic consideration of the Legislature. The present system has never been exempt from serious and weighty objections. The idea of appealing from the circuit court to the same judges in the Supreme Court is recommended by little hopes of redress to the injured party below. The duties of the circuit, too, it may be added, consume one half of the year, leaving a small and inadequate portion of time (when that required for domestic purposes is deducted) to erect, in the decisions of the Supreme Court, a judicial monument of legal learning and research, which the talent and ability of the court might otherwise be entirely competent to."

With this organization of circuit courts the people have never complained. The only complaints which we have heard have come from circuits which were so large that the judges could not dispose of the business, and the circuits in which Judges Pearson and Ralston lately presided.

Whilst the honor and credit of the State demanded legislation upon the subject of the public debt, the canal, the unfinished public works, and the embarrassments of the people, the judiciary stood upon a basis which required no change—no legislative action. Yet the party in power, neglecting every interest requiring legislative action, and wholly disregarding the rights, wishes, and interests of the people, has, for the unholy purpose of providing places for its partisans and supplying them with large salaries, disorganized that department of the government. Provision is made for the election of five party judges of the Supreme Court, the proscription of four circuit judges, and the appointment of party clerks in more than half the counties of the State. Men professing respect for public opinion, and acknowledged to be leaders of the party, have avowed in the halls of legislation that the change in the judiciary was intended to produce political results favorable to their party and party friends. The immutable principles of justice are to make way for party interests, and the bonds of social order are to be rent in twain, in order that a desperate faction may be sustained at the expense of the people. The change proposed in the judiciary was supported upon grounds so destructive to the institutions of the country, and so entirely at war with the rights and liberties of the people, that the party could not secure entire unanimity in its support, three Democrats of the Senate and five of the House voting against the measure. They were unwilling to see the temples of justice and the seats of independent judges occupied by the tools of faction. The declarations of the party leaders, the selection of party men for judges, and the total disregard for the public will in the adoption of the measure, prove conclusively that the object has been not reform, but destruction; not the advancement of the highest interests of the State, but the predominance of party.

We cannot in this manner undertake to point out all the objections to this party measure; we present you with those stated by the Council of Revision upon returning the bill, and we ask for them a candid consideration.

Believing that the independence of the judiciary has been destroyed, that hereafter our courts will be independent of the people, and entirely dependent upon the Legislature; that our rights of property and liberty of conscience can no longer be regarded as safe from the encroachments of unconstitutional legislation; and knowing of no other remedy which can be adopted consistently with the peace and good order of society, we call upon you to avail yourselves of the opportunity afforded, and, at the next general election, vote for a convention of the people.

S. H. LITTLE,
E. D. BAKER,
J. J. HARDIN,

E. B. WEBS,
A. LINCOLN,
J. GILLESPIE,

Committee on behalf of the Whig members of the Legislature.

AGAINST THE REORGANIZATION OF THE JUDICIARY.
EXTRACT FROM A PROTEST IN THE ILLINOIS LEGISLATURE

February 26, 1841

For the reasons thus presented, and for others no less apparent, the undersigned cannot assent to the passage of the bill, or permit it to become a law, without this evidence of their disapprobation; and they now protest against the reorganization of the judiciary, because—(1) It violates the great principles of free government by subjecting the judiciary to the Legislature. (2) It is a fatal blow at the independence of the judges and the constitutional term of their office. (3) It is a measure not asked for, or wished for, by the people. (4) It will greatly increase the expense of our courts, or else greatly diminish their utility. (5) It will give our courts a political and partisan character, thereby impairing public confidence in their decisions. (6) It will impair our standing with other States and the world. (7)It is a party measure for party purposes, from which no practical good to the people can possibly arise, but which may be the source of immeasurable evils.

The undersigned are well aware that this protest will be altogether unavailing with the majority of this body. The blow has already fallen, and we are compelled to stand by, the mournful spectators of the ruin it will cause.

[Signed by 35 members, among whom was Abraham Lincoln.]

TO JOSHUA F. SPEED—MURDER CASE
SPRINGFIELD June 19, 1841.

DEAR SPEED:—We have had the highest state of excitement here for a week past that our community has ever witnessed; and, although the public feeling is somewhat allayed, the curious affair which aroused it is very far from being even yet cleared of mystery. It would take a quire of paper to give you anything like a full account of it, and I therefore only propose a brief outline. The chief personages in the drama are Archibald Fisher, supposed to be murdered, and Archibald Trailor, Henry Trailor, and William Trailor, supposed to have murdered him. The three Trailors are brothers: the first, Arch., as you know, lives in town; the second, Henry, in Clary's Grove; and the third, William, in Warren County; and Fisher, the supposed murdered, being without a family, had made his home with William. On Saturday evening, being the 29th of May, Fisher and William came to Henry's in a one-horse dearborn, and there stayed over Sunday; and on Monday all three came to Springfield (Henry on horseback) and joined Archibald at Myers's, the Dutch carpenter. That evening at supper Fisher was missing, and so next morning some ineffectual search was made for him; and on Tuesday, at one o'clock P.M., William and Henry started home without him. In a day or two Henry and one or two of his Clary-Grove neighbors came back for him again, and advertised his disappearance in the papers. The knowledge of the matter thus far had not been general, and here it dropped entirely, till about the 10th instant, when Keys received a letter from the postmaster in Warren County, that William had arrived at home, and was telling a very mysterious and improbable story about the disappearance of Fisher, which induced the community there to suppose he had been disposed of unfairly. Keys made this letter public, which immediately set the whole town and adjoining county agog. And so it has continued until yesterday. The mass of the people commenced a systematic search for the dead body, while Wickersham was despatched to arrest Henry Trailor at the Grove, and Jim Maxcy to Warren to arrest William. On Monday last, Henry was brought in, and showed an evident inclination to insinuate that he knew Fisher to be dead, and that Arch. and William had killed him. He said he guessed the body could be found in Spring Creek, between the Beardstown road and Hickox's mill. Away the people swept like a herd of buffalo, and cut down Hickox's mill-dam nolens volens, to draw the water out of the pond, and then went up and down and down and up the creek, fishing and raking, and raking and ducking and diving for two days, and, after all, no dead body found.

In the meantime a sort of scuffling-ground had been found in the brush in the angle, or point, where the road leading into the woods past the brewery and the one leading in past the brick-yard meet. From the scuffle-ground was the sign of something about the size of a man having been dragged to the edge of the thicket, where it joined the track of some small-wheeled carriage drawn by one horse, as shown by the road-tracks. The carriage-track led off toward Spring Creek. Near this drag-trail Dr. Merryman found two hairs, which, after a long scientific examination, he pronounced to be triangular human hairs, which term, he says, includes within it the whiskers, the hair growing under the arms and on other parts of the body; and he judged that these two were of the whiskers, because the ends were cut, showing that they had flourished in the neighborhood of the razor's operations. On Thursday last Jim Maxcy brought in William Trailor from Warren. On the same day Arch. was arrested and put in jail. Yesterday (Friday) William was put upon his examining trial before May and Lovely. Archibald and Henry were both present. Lamborn prosecuted, and Logan, Baker, and your humble servant defended. A great many witnesses were introduced and examined, but I shall only mention those whose testimony seemed most important. The first of these was Captain Ransdell. He swore that when William and Henry left Springfield for home on Tuesday before mentioned they did not take the direct route,—which, you know, leads by the butcher shop,—but that they followed the street north until they got opposite, or nearly opposite, May's new house, after which he could not see them from where he stood; and it was afterwards proved that in about an hour after they started, they came into the street by the butcher shop from toward the brickyard. Dr. Merryman and others swore to what is stated about the scuffle-ground, drag-trail, whiskers, and carriage tracks. Henry was then introduced by the prosecution. He swore that when they started for home they went out north, as Ransdell stated, and turned down west by the brick-yard into the woods, and there met Archibald; that they proceeded a small distance farther, when he was placed as a sentinel to watch for and announce the approach of any one that might happen that way; that William and Arch. took the dearborn out of the road a small distance to the edge of the thicket, where they

142

stopped, and he saw them lift the body of a man into it; that they then moved off with the carriage in the direction of Hickox's mill, and he loitered about for something like an hour, when William returned with the carriage, but without Arch., and said they had put him in a safe place; that they went somehow he did not know exactly how—into the road close to the brewery, and proceeded on to Clary's Grove. He also stated that some time during the day William told him that he and Arch. had killed Fisher the evening before; that the way they did it was by him William knocking him down with a club, and Arch. then choking him to death.

An old man from Warren, called Dr. Gilmore, was then introduced on the part of the defense. He swore that he had known Fisher for several years; that Fisher had resided at his house a long time at each of two different spells—once while he built a barn for him, and once while he was doctored for some chronic disease; that two or three years ago Fisher had a serious hurt in his head by the bursting of a gun, since which he had been subject to continued bad health and occasional aberration of mind. He also stated that on last Tuesday, being the same day that Maxcy arrested William Trailor, he (the doctor) was from home in the early part of the day, and on his return, about eleven o'clock, found Fisher at his house in bed, and apparently very unwell; that he asked him how he came from Springfield; that Fisher said he had come by Peoria, and also told of several other places he had been at more in the direction of Peoria, which showed that he at the time of speaking did not know where he had been wandering about in a state of derangement. He further stated that in about two hours he received a note from one of Trailor's friends, advising him of his arrest, and requesting him to go on to Springfield as a witness, to testify as to the state of Fisher's health in former times; that he immediately set off, calling up two of his neighbors as company, and, riding all evening and all night, overtook Maxcy and William at Lewiston in Fulton County; that Maxcy refusing to discharge Trailor upon his statement, his two neighbors returned and he came on to Springfield. Some question being made as to whether the doctor's story was not a fabrication, several acquaintances of his (among whom was the same postmaster who wrote Keys, as before mentioned) were introduced as sort of compurgators, who swore that they knew the doctor to be of good character for truth and veracity, and generally of good character in every way.

Here the testimony ended, and the Trailors were discharged, Arch. and William expressing both in word and manner their entire confidence that Fisher would be found alive at the doctor's by Galloway, Mallory, and Myers, who a day before had been despatched for that purpose; which Henry still protested that no power on earth could ever show Fisher alive. Thus stands this curious affair. When the doctor's story was first made public, it was amusing to scan and contemplate the countenances and hear the remarks of those who had been actively in search for the dead body: some looked quizzical, some melancholy, and some furiously angry. Porter, who had been very active, swore he always knew the man was not dead, and that he had not stirred an inch to hunt for him; Langford, who had taken the lead in cutting down Hickox's mill-dam, and wanted to hang Hickox for objecting, looked most awfully woebegone: he seemed the "victim of unrequited affection," as represented in the comic almanacs we used to laugh over; and Hart, the little drayman that hauled Molly home once, said it was too damned bad to have so much trouble, and no hanging after all.

I commenced this letter on yesterday, since which I received yours of the 13th. I stick to my promise to come to Louisville. Nothing new here except what I have written. I have not seen _____ since my last trip, and I am going out there as soon as I mail this letter.

Yours forever, LINCOLN.

STATEMENT ABOUT HARRY WILTON.
June 25, 1841

It having been charged in some of the public prints that Harry Wilton, late United States marshal for the district of Illinois, had used his office for political effect, in the appointment of deputies for the taking of the census for the year 1840, we, the undersigned, were called upon by Mr. Wilton to examine the papers in his possession relative to these appointments, and to ascertain therefrom the correctness or incorrectness of such charge. We accompanied Mr. Wilton to a room, and examined the matter as fully as we could with the means afforded us. The only sources of information bearing on the subject which were submitted to us were the letters, etc., recommending and opposing the various appointments made, and Mr.

Wilton's verbal statements concerning the same. From these letters, etc., it appears that in some instances appointments were made in accordance with the recommendations of leading Whigs, and in opposition to those of leading Democrats; among which instances the appointments at Scott, Wayne, Madison, and Lawrence are the strongest. According to Mr. Wilton's statement of the seventy-six appointments we examined, fifty-four were of Democrats, eleven of Whigs, and eleven of unknown politics.

The chief ground of complaint against Mr. Wilton, as we had understood it, was because of his appointment of so many Democratic candidates for the Legislature, thus giving them a decided advantage over their Whig opponents; and consequently our attention was directed rather particularly to that point. We found that there were many such appointments, among which were those in Tazewell, McLean, Iroquois, Coles, Menard, Wayne, Washington, Fayette, etc.; and we did not learn that there was one instance in which a Whig candidate for the Legislature had been appointed. There was no written evidence before us showing us at what time those appointments were made; but Mr. Wilton stated that they all with one exception were made before those appointed became candidates for the Legislature, and the letters, etc., recommending them all bear date before, and most of them long before, those appointed were publicly announced candidates.

We give the foregoing naked facts and draw no conclusions from them.

BEND. S. EDWARDS, A. LINCOLN.

TO MISS MARY SPEED—PRACTICAL SLAVERY
BLOOMINGTON, ILL.,
September 27, 1841.

Miss Mary Speed, Louisville, Ky.

MY FRIEND: By the way, a fine example was presented on board the boat for contemplating the effect of condition upon human happiness. A gentleman had purchased twelve negroes in different parts of Kentucky, and was taking them to a farm in the South. They were chained six and six together. A small iron clevis was around the left wrist of each, and this fastened to the main chain by a shorter one, at a convenient distance from the others, so that the negroes were strung together precisely like so many fish upon a trotline. In this condition they were being separated forever from the scenes of their childhood, their friends, their fathers and mothers, and brothers and sisters, and many of them from their wives and children, and going into perpetual slavery where the lash of the master is proverbially more ruthless and unrelenting than any other; and yet amid all these distressing circumstances, as we would think them, they were the most cheerful and apparently happy creatures on board. One, whose offence for which he had been sold was an overfondness for his wife, played the fiddle almost continually, and the others danced, sang, cracked jokes, and played various games with cards from day to day. How true it is that 'God tempers the wind to the shorn lamb,' or in other words, that he renders the worst of human conditions tolerable, while he permits the best to be nothing better than tolerable. To return to the narrative: When we reached Springfield I stayed but one day, when I started on this tedious circuit where I now am. Do you remember my going to the city, while I was in Kentucky, to have a tooth extracted, and making a failure of it? Well, that same old tooth got to paining me so much that about a week since I had it torn out, bringing with it a bit of the jawbone, the consequence of which is that my mouth is now so sore that I can neither talk nor eat.

Your sincere friend, A. LINCOLN.

1842

TO JOSHUA F. SPEED—ON MARRIAGE
January 30, 1842.

MY DEAR SPEED:—Feeling, as you know I do, the deepest solicitude for the success of the enterprise you are engaged in, I adopt this as the last method I can adopt to aid you, in case (which God forbid!) you shall need any aid. I do not place what I am going to say on paper because I can say it better that way than I could by word of mouth, but, were I to say it orally before we part, most likely you would forget it at the very time when it might do you some good. As I think it reasonable that you will feel very badly some time between this and the final consummation of your purpose, it is intended that you shall read this just at such a time. Why I say it is reasonable that you will feel very badly yet, is because of three special causes added to the general one which I shall mention.

The general cause is, that you are naturally of a nervous temperament; and this I say from what I have seen of you personally, and what you have told me concerning your mother at various times, and concerning your brother William at the time his wife died. The first special cause is your exposure to bad weather on your journey, which my experience clearly proves to be very severe on defective nerves. The second is the absence of all business and conversation of friends, which might divert your mind, give it occasional rest from the intensity of thought which will sometimes wear the sweetest idea threadbare and turn it to the bitterness of death. The third is the rapid and near approach of that crisis on which all your thoughts and feelings concentrate.

If from all these causes you shall escape and go through triumphantly, without another "twinge of the soul," I shall be most happily but most egregiously deceived. If, on the contrary, you shall, as I expect you will at sometime, be agonized and distressed, let me, who have some reason to speak with judgment on such a subject, beseech you to ascribe it to the causes I have mentioned, and not to some false and ruinous suggestion of the Devil.

"But," you will say, "do not your causes apply to every one engaged in a like undertaking?" By no means. The particular causes, to a greater or less extent, perhaps do apply in all cases; but the general one,—nervous debility, which is the key and conductor of all the particular ones, and without which they would be utterly harmless,— though it does pertain to you, does not pertain to one in a thousand. It is out of this that the painful difference between you and the mass of the world springs.

I know what the painful point with you is at all times when you are unhappy; it is an apprehension that you do not love her as you should. What nonsense! How came you to court her? Was it because you thought she deserved it, and that you had given her reason to expect it? If it was for that why did not the same reason make you court Ann

147

Todd, and at least twenty others of whom you can think, and to whom it would apply with greater force than to her? Did you court her for her wealth? Why, you know she had none. But you say you reasoned yourself into it. What do you mean by that? Was it not that you found yourself unable to reason yourself out of it? Did you not think, and partly form the purpose, of courting her the first time you ever saw her or heard of her? What had reason to do with it at that early stage? There was nothing at that time for reason to work upon. Whether she was moral, amiable, sensible, or even of good character, you did not, nor could then know, except, perhaps, you might infer the last from the company you found her in.

All you then did or could know of her was her personal appearance and deportment; and these, if they impress at all, impress the heart, and not the head.

Say candidly, were not those heavenly black eyes the whole basis of all your early reasoning on the subject? After you and I had once been at the residence, did you not go and take me all the way to Lexington and back, for no other purpose but to get to see her again, on our return on that evening to take a trip for that express object? What earthly consideration would you take to find her scouting and despising you, and giving herself up to another? But of this you have no apprehension; and therefore you cannot bring it home to your feelings.

I shall be so anxious about you that I shall want you to write by every mail.

Your friend, LINCOLN.

TO JOSHUA F. SPEED.
SPRINGFIELD, ILLINOIS,
February 3, 1842.

DEAR SPEED:—Your letter of the 25th January came to hand to-day. You well know that I do not feel my own sorrows much more keenly than I do yours, when I know of them; and yet I assure you I was not much hurt by what you wrote me of your excessively bad feeling at the time you wrote. Not that I am less capable of sympathizing with you now than ever, not that I am less your friend than ever, but because I hope and believe that your present anxiety and distress about her health and her life must and will forever banish those horrid doubts which I know you sometimes felt as to the truth of your affection for her. If they can once and forever be removed (and I almost feel a presentiment that the Almighty has sent your present affliction expressly for that object), surely nothing can come in their stead to fill their immeasurable measure of misery. The death-scenes of those we love are surely painful enough; but these we are prepared for and expect to see: they happen to all, and all know they must happen. Painful as they are, they are not an unlooked for sorrow. Should she, as you fear, be destined to an early grave, it is indeed a great consolation to know that she is so well prepared to meet it. Her religion, which you once disliked so much, I will venture you now prize most highly. But I hope your melancholy bodings as to her early death are not well founded. I even hope that ere this reaches you she will have returned with improved and still improving health, and that you will have met her, and forgotten the sorrows of the past in the enjoyments of the present. I would say more if I could, but it seems that I have said enough. It really appears to me that you yourself ought to rejoice, and not sorrow, at this indubitable evidence of your undying affection for her. Why, Speed, if you did not love her although you might not wish her death, you would most certainly be resigned to it. Perhaps this point is no longer a question with you, and my pertinacious dwelling upon it is a rude intrusion upon your feelings. If so, you must pardon me. You know the hell I have suffered on that point, and how tender I am upon it. You know I do not mean wrong. I have been quite clear of "hypo" since you left, even better than I was along in the fall. I have seen _____ but once. She seemed very cheerful, and so I said nothing to her about what we spoke of.

Old Uncle Billy Herndon is dead, and it is said this evening that Uncle Ben Ferguson will not live. This, I believe, is all the news, and enough at that unless it were better. Write me immediately on the receipt of this.

Your friend, as ever, LINCOLN.

TO JOSHUA F. SPEED—ON DEPRESSION SPRINGFIELD, ILLINOIS, February 13, 1842.

DEAR SPEED:—Yours of the 1st instant came to hand three or four days ago. When this shall reach you, you will have been Fanny's husband several days. You know my desire to befriend you is everlasting; that I will never cease while I know how to do anything. But you will always hereafter be on ground that I have never occupied, and consequently, if advice were needed, I might advise wrong. I do fondly hope, however, that you will never again need any comfort from abroad. But should I be mistaken in this, should excessive pleasure still be accompanied with a painful counterpart at times, still let me urge you, as I have ever done, to remember, in the depth and even agony of despondency, that very shortly you are to feel well again. I am now fully convinced that you love her as ardently as you are capable of loving. Your ever being happy in her presence, and your intense anxiety about her health, if there were nothing else, would place this beyond all dispute in my mind. I incline to think it probable that your nerves will fail you occasionally for a while; but once you get them firmly guarded now that trouble is over forever. I think, if I were you, in case my mind were not exactly right, I would avoid being idle. I would immediately engage in some business, or go to making preparations for it, which would be the same thing. If you went through the ceremony calmly, or even with sufficient composure not to excite alarm in any present, you are safe beyond question, and in two or three months, to say the most, will be the happiest of men.

I would desire you to give my particular respects to Fanny; but perhaps you will not wish her to know you have received this, lest she should desire to see it. Make her write me an answer to my last letter to her; at any rate I would set great value upon a note or letter from her. Write me whenever you have leisure. Yours forever, A. LINCOLN. P. S.—I have been quite a man since you left.

TO G. B. SHELEDY.
SPRINGFIELD, ILL., Feb. 16, 1842.

G. B. SHELEDY, ESQ.:

Yours of the 10th is duly received. Judge Logan and myself are doing business together now, and we are willing to attend to your cases as you propose. As to the terms, we are willing to attend each case you prepare and send us for $10 (when there shall be no opposition) to be sent in advance, or you to know that it is safe. It takes $5.75 of cost to start upon, that is, $1.75 to clerk, and $2 to each of two publishers of papers. Judge Logan thinks it will take the balance of $20 to carry a case through. This must be advanced from time to time as the services are performed, as the officers will not act without. I do not know whether you can be admitted an attorney of the Federal court in your absence or not; nor is it material, as the business can be done in our names.

Thinking it may aid you a little, I send you one of our blank forms of Petitions. It, you will see, is framed to be sworn to before the Federal court clerk, and, in your cases, will have [to] be so far changed as to be sworn to before the clerk of your circuit court; and his certificate must be accompanied with his official seal. The schedules, too, must be attended to. Be sure that they contain the creditors' names, their residences, the amounts due each, the debtors' names, their residences, and the amounts they owe, also all property and where located.

Also be sure that the schedules are all signed by the applicants as well as the Petition. Publication will have to be made here in one paper, and in one nearest the residence of the applicant. Write us in each case where the last advertisement is to be sent, whether to you or to what paper.

I believe I have now said everything that can be of any advantage. Your friend as ever, A. LINCOLN.

TO GEORGE E. PICKETT—ADVICE TO YOUTH, February 22, 1842.

I never encourage deceit, and falsehood, especially if you have got a bad memory, is the worst enemy a fellow can have. The fact is truth is your truest friend, no matter what the circumstances are. Notwithstanding this copy-book preamble, my boy, I am inclined to suggest a little prudence on your part. You see I have a congenital aversion to failure, and the sudden announcement to your Uncle Andrew of the success of your "lamp rubbing" might possibly prevent your passing the severe physical examination to which you will be subjected in order to enter the Military Academy. You see I should like to have a perfect soldier credited to dear old Illinois—no broken bones, scalp wounds, etc. So I think it might be wise to hand this letter from me in to your good uncle through his room-window after he has had a comfortable dinner, and watch its effect from the top of the pigeon-house.

I have just told the folks here in Springfield on this 111th anniversary of the birth of him whose name, mightiest in the cause of civil liberty, still mightiest in the cause of moral reformation, we mention in solemn awe, in naked, deathless splendor, that the one victory we can ever call complete will be that one which proclaims that there is not one slave or one drunkard on the face of God's green earth. Recruit for this victory.

Now, boy, on your march, don't you go and forget the old maxim that "one drop of honey catches more flies than a half-gallon of gall." Load your musket with this maxim, and smoke it in your pipe.

ADDRESS BEFORE THE SPRINGFIELD WASHINGTONIAN TEMPERANCE SOCIETY, FEBRUARY 22, 1842.

Although the temperance cause has been in progress for near twenty years, it is apparent to all that it is just now being crowned with a degree of success hitherto unparalleled.

The list of its friends is daily swelled by the additions of fifties, of hundreds, and of thousands. The cause itself seems suddenly transformed from a cold abstract theory to a living, breathing, active, and powerful chieftain, going forth "conquering and to conquer." The citadels of his great adversary are daily being stormed and dismantled; his temple and his altars, where the rites of his idolatrous worship have long been performed, and where human sacrifices have long been wont to be made, are daily desecrated and deserted. The triumph of the conqueror's fame is sounding from hill to hill, from sea to sea, and from land to land, and calling millions to his standard at a blast.

For this new and splendid success we heartily rejoice. That that success is so much greater now than heretofore is doubtless owing to rational causes; and if we would have it continue, we shall do well to inquire what those causes are.

The warfare heretofore waged against the demon intemperance has somehow or other been erroneous. Either the champions engaged or the tactics they adopted have not been the most proper. These champions for the most part have been preachers, lawyers, and hired agents. Between these and the mass of mankind there is a want of approachability, if the term be admissible, partially, at least, fatal to their success. They are supposed to have no sympathy of feeling or interest with those very persons whom it is their object to convince and persuade.

And again, it is so common and so easy to ascribe motives to men of these classes other than those they profess to act upon. The preacher, it is said, advocates temperance because he is a fanatic, and desires a union of the Church and State; the lawyer from his pride and vanity of hearing himself speak; and the hired agent for his salary. But when one who has long been known as a victim of intemperance bursts the fetters that have bound him, and appears before his neighbors "clothed and in his right mind," a redeemed specimen of long-lost humanity, and stands up, with tears of joy trembling in his eyes, to tell of the miseries once endured, now to be endured no more forever; of his once naked and starving children, now clad and fed comfortably; of a wife long weighed down with woe, weeping, and a broken heart, now restored to health, happiness, and a renewed affection; and how easily it is all done, once it is resolved to be done; how simple his language! there is a logic and an eloquence in it that few with human feelings can resist. They cannot say that he desires a union of Church and State, for he is not a church member; they cannot say he is vain of hearing himself speak, for his whole demeanor shows he would gladly avoid speaking at all; they cannot say he speaks for pay, for he receives none, and asks for none. Nor can his sincerity in any way be doubted, or his sympathy for those he would persuade to imitate his example be denied.

In my judgment, it is to the battles of this new class of champions that our late success is greatly, perhaps chiefly, owing. But, had the old-school champions themselves been of the most wise selecting, was their system of tactics the most judicious? It seems to me it was not. Too much denunciation against dram-sellers and dram-drinkers was indulged in. This I think was both impolitic and unjust. It was impolitic, because it is not much in the nature of man to be driven to anything; still less to be driven about that which is exclusively his own business; and least of all where such driving is to be submitted to at the expense of pecuniary interest or burning appetite. When the dram-seller and drinker were incessantly told not in accents of entreaty and persuasion, diffidently addressed by erring man to an erring brother, but in the thundering tones of anathema and denunciation with which the lordly judge often groups together all the crimes of the felon's life, and thrusts them in his face just ere he passes sentence of death upon him that they were the authors of all the vice and misery and crime in the land; that they were the manufacturers and material of all the thieves and robbers and murderers that infest the earth; that their houses were the workshops of the devil; and that their persons should be shunned by all the good and virtuous, as moral pestilences—I say, when they were told all this, and in this way, it is not wonderful that they were slow to acknowledge the truth of such denunciations, and to join the ranks of their denouncers in a hue and cry against themselves.

To have expected them to do otherwise than they did to have expected them not to meet denunciation with denunciation, crimination with crimination, and anathema with anathema—was to expect a reversal of human nature, which is God's decree and can never be reversed.

When the conduct of men is designed to be influenced, persuasion, kind, unassuming persuasion, should ever be adopted. It is an old and a true maxim that "a drop of honey catches more flies than a gallon of gall." So with men. If you would win a man to your cause, first convince him that you are his sincere friend. Therein is a drop of honey that catches his heart, which, say what he will, is the great highroad to his reason; and which, when once gained, you will find but little trouble in convincing his judgment of the justice of your cause, if indeed that cause really be a just one. On the contrary, assume to dictate to his judgment, or to command his action, or to mark him as one to be shunned and despised, and he will retreat within himself, close all the avenues to his head and his heart; and though your cause be naked truth itself, transformed to the heaviest lance, harder than steel, and sharper than steel can be made, and though you throw it with more than herculean force and precision, you shall be no more able to pierce him than to penetrate the hard shell of a tortoise with a rye straw. Such is man, and so must he be understood by those who would lead him, even to his own best interests.

On this point the Washingtonians greatly excel the temperance advocates of former times. Those whom they desire to convince and persuade are their old friends and companions. They know they are not demons, nor even the worst of men; they know that generally they are kind, generous, and charitable even beyond the example of their more staid and sober neighbors. They are practical philanthropists; and they glow with a generous and brotherly zeal that mere theorizers are incapable of feeling. Benevolence and charity possess their hearts entirely; and out of the abundance of their hearts their tongues give utterance; "love through all their actions runs, and all their words are mild." In this spirit they speak and act, and in the same they are heard and regarded. And when such is the temper of the advocate, and such of the audience, no good cause can be unsuccessful. But I have said that denunciations against dramsellers and dram-drinkers are unjust, as well as impolitic. Let us see. I have not inquired at what period of time the use of intoxicating liquors commenced; nor is it important to know. It is sufficient that, to all of us who now inhabit the world, the practice of drinking them is just as old as the world itself that is, we have seen the one just as long as we have seen the other. When all such of us as have now reached the years of maturity first opened our eyes upon the stage of existence, we found intoxicating liquor recognized by everybody, used by everybody, repudiated by nobody. It commonly entered into the first draught of the infant and the last draught of the dying man. From the sideboard of the parson down to the ragged pocket of the houseless loafer, it was constantly found. Physicians proscribed it in this, that, and the other disease; government provided it for soldiers and sailors; and to have a rolling or raising, a husking or "hoedown," anywhere about without it was positively insufferable. So, too, it was everywhere a respectable article of manufacture and merchandise. The making of it was regarded as an honorable livelihood, and he who could make most was the most enterprising and respectable. Large and small manufactories of it were everywhere erected, in which all the earthly goods of their owners were invested. Wagons drew it from town to town; boats bore it from clime to clime, and the winds wafted it from nation to nation; and merchants bought and sold it, by wholesale and retail, with precisely the same feelings on the part of the seller, buyer, and bystander as are felt at the selling and buying of ploughs, beef, bacon, or any other of the real necessaries of life. Universal public opinion not only tolerated but recognized and adopted its use.

It is true that even then it was known and acknowledged that many were greatly injured by it; but none seemed to think the injury arose from the use of a bad thing, but from the abuse of a very good thing. The victims of it were to be pitied and compassionated, just as are the heirs of consumption and other hereditary diseases. Their failing was treated as a misfortune, and not as a crime, or even as a disgrace. If, then, what I have been saying is true, is it wonderful that some should think and act now as all thought and acted twenty years ago? and is it just to assail, condemn, or despise them for doing so? The universal sense of mankind on any subject is an argument, or at least an influence, not easily overcome. The success of the argument in favor of the existence of an overruling Providence mainly depends upon that sense; and men ought not in justice to be denounced for yielding to it in any case, or giving it up slowly, especially when they are backed by interest, fixed habits, or burning appetites.

Another error, as it seems to me, into which the old reformers fell, was the position that all habitual drunkards were utterly incorrigible, and therefore must be turned adrift and damned without remedy in order that the grace of temperance might abound, to the temperate then, and to all mankind some hundreds of years thereafter. There is in this some thing so repugnant to humanity, so uncharitable, so cold-blooded and feelingless, that it, never did nor ever can enlist the enthusiasm of a popular cause. We could not love the man who taught it we could not hear him with patience. The heart could not throw open its portals to it, the generous man could not adopt it—it could not mix with his blood. It looked so fiendishly selfish, so like throwing fathers and brothers overboard to lighten the boat for our security, that the noble-minded shrank from the manifest meanness of the thing. And besides this, the benefits of a reformation to be effected by such a system were too remote in point of time to warmly engage many in its behalf. Few can be induced to labor exclusively for posterity, and none

156

will do it enthusiastically. —Posterity has done nothing for us; and, theorize on it as we may, practically we shall do very little for it, unless we are made to think we are at the same time doing something for ourselves.

What an ignorance of human nature does it exhibit to ask or to expect a whole community to rise up and labor for the temporal happiness of others, after themselves shall be consigned to the dust, a majority of which community take no pains whatever to secure their own eternal welfare at no more distant day! Great distance in either time or space has wonderful power to lull and render quiescent the human mind. Pleasures to be enjoyed, or pains to be endured, after we shall be dead and gone are but little regarded even in our own cases, and much less in the cases of others. Still, in addition to this there is something so ludicrous in promises of good or threats of evil a great way off as to render the whole subject with which they are connected easily turned into ridicule. "Better lay down that spade you are stealing, Paddy; if you don't you'll pay for it at the day of judgment." "Be the powers, if ye'll credit me so long I'll take another jist."

By the Washingtonians this system of consigning the habitual drunkard to hopeless ruin is repudiated. They adopt a more enlarged philanthropy; they go for present as well as future good. They labor for all now living, as well as hereafter to live. They teach hope to all-despair to none. As applying to their cause, they deny the doctrine of unpardonable sin; as in Christianity it is taught, so in this they teach— "While—While the lamp holds out to burn, The vilest sinner may return." And, what is a matter of more profound congratulation, they, by experiment upon experiment and example upon example, prove the maxim to be no less true in the one case than in the other. On every hand we behold those who but yesterday were the chief of sinners, now the chief apostles of the cause. Drunken devils are cast out by ones, by sevens, by legions; and their unfortunate victims, like the poor possessed who were redeemed from their long and lonely wanderings in the tombs, are publishing to the ends of the earth how great things have been done for them.

To these new champions and this new system of tactics our late success is mainly owing, and to them we must mainly look for the final consummation. The ball is now rolling gloriously on, and none are so able as they to increase its speed and its bulk, to add to its momentum and its magnitude—even though unlearned in letters, for this task none are so well educated. To fit them for this work they have been taught in the true school. They have been in that gulf from which they would teach others the means of escape. They have passed that prison wall which others have long declared impassable; and who that has not shall dare to weigh opinions with them as to the mode of passing?

But if it be true, as I have insisted, that those who have suffered by intemperance personally, and have reformed, are the most powerful and efficient instruments to push the reformation to ultimate success, it does not follow that those who have not suffered have no part left them to perform. Whether or not the world would be vastly benefited by a total and final banishment from it of all intoxicating drinks seems to me not now an open question. Three fourths of mankind confess the affirmative with their tongues, and, I believe, all the rest acknowledge it in their hearts.

Ought any, then, to refuse their aid in doing what good the good of the whole demands? Shall he who cannot do much be for that reason excused if he do nothing? "But," says one, "what good can I do by signing the pledge? I never drank, even without signing." This question has already been asked and answered more than a million of times. Let it be answered once more. For the man suddenly or in any other way to break off from the use of drams, who has indulged in them for a long course of years and until his appetite for them has grown ten or a hundredfold stronger and more craving than any natural appetite can be, requires a most powerful moral effort. In such an undertaking he needs every moral support and influence that can possibly be brought to his aid and thrown around him. And not only so, but every moral prop should be taken from whatever argument might rise in his mind to lure him to his backsliding. When he casts his eyes around him, he should be able to see all that he respects, all that he admires, all that he loves, kindly and anxiously pointing him onward, and none beckoning him back to his former miserable "wallowing in the mire."

But it is said by some that men will think and act for themselves; that none will disuse spirits or anything else because his neighbors do; and that moral influence is not that powerful engine contended for. Let us examine this. Let me ask the man who could maintain this position most stiffly, what compensation he will accept to go to church some Sunday and sit during the sermon with his wife's bonnet upon his head? Not a trifle, I'll venture. And why not? There would be nothing irreligious in it, nothing immoral, nothing uncomfortable—then why not? Is it not because there would be something egregiously unfashionable in it? Then it is the influence of fashion; and what is the influence of fashion but the influence that other people's actions have on our actions—the strong inclination each of us feels to do as we see all our neighbors do? Nor is the influence of fashion confined to any particular thing or class of things; it is just as strong on one subject as another. Let us make it as unfashionable to withhold our names from the temperance cause as for husbands to wear their wives' bonnets to church, and instances will be just as rare in the one case as the other.

"But," say some, "we are no drunkards, and we shall not acknowledge ourselves such by joining a reformed drunkard's society, whatever our influence might be." Surely no Christian will adhere to this objection. If they believe as they profess, that Omnipotence condescended to take on himself the form of sinful man, and as such to die an ignominious death for their sakes, surely they will not refuse submission to the infinitely lesser condescension, for the temporal, and perhaps eternal, salvation of a large, erring, and unfortunate class of their fellow-creatures. Nor is the condescension very great. In my judgment such of us as have never fallen victims have been spared more by the absence of appetite than from any mental or moral superiority over those who have. Indeed, I believe if we take habitual drunkards as a class, their heads and their hearts will bear an advantageous comparison with those of any other class. There seems ever to have been a proneness in the brilliant and warm-blooded to fall into this vice—the demon of intemperance ever seems to have delighted in sucking the blood of genius and of generosity. What one of us but can call to mind some relative, more promising in youth than all his fellows, who has fallen a sacrifice to his rapacity? He ever seems to have gone forth like the Egyptian angel of death, commissioned to slay, if not the first, the fairest born of every family. Shall he now be arrested in his desolating career? In that arrest all can give aid that will; and who shall be excused that can and will not? Far around as human breath has ever blown he keeps our fathers, our brothers, our sons, and our friends prostrate in the chains of moral death. To all the living everywhere we cry, "Come sound the moral trump, that these may rise and stand up an exceeding great army." "Come from the four winds, O breath! and breathe upon these slain that they may live." If the relative grandeur of revolutions shall be estimated by the great amount of human misery they alleviate, and the small amount they inflict, then indeed will this be the grandest the world shall ever have seen.

Of our political revolution of '76 we are all justly proud. It has given us a degree of political freedom far exceeding that of any other nation of the earth. In it the world has found a solution of the long-mooted problem as to the capability of man to govern himself. In it was the germ which has vegetated, and still is to grow and expand into the universal liberty of mankind. But, with all these glorious results, past, present, and to come, it had its evils too. It breathed forth famine, swam in blood, and rode in fire; and long, long after, the orphan's cry and the widow's wail continued to break the sad silence that ensued. These were the price, the inevitable price, paid for the blessings it bought.

Turn now to the temperance revolution. In it we shall find a stronger bondage broken, a viler slavery manumitted, a greater tyrant deposed; in it, more of want supplied, more disease healed, more sorrow assuaged. By it no Orphans starving, no widows weeping. By it none wounded in feeling, none injured in interest; even the drammaker and dram-seller will have glided into other occupations so gradually as never to have felt the change, and will stand ready to join all others in the universal song of gladness. And what a noble ally this to the cause of political freedom, with such an aid its march cannot fail to be on and on, till every son of earth shall drink in rich fruition the sorrow-quenching draughts of perfect liberty. Happy day when-all appetites controlled, all poisons subdued, all matter subjected-mind, all-conquering mind, shall live and move, the monarch of the world. Glorious consummation! Hail, fall of fury! Reign of reason, all hail!

And when the victory shall be complete, when there shall be neither a slave nor a drunkard on the earth, how proud the title of that land which may truly claim to be the birthplace and the cradle of both those revolutions that shall have ended in that victory. How nobly distinguished that people who shall have planted and nurtured to maturity both the political and moral freedom of their species.

This is the one hundred and tenth anniversary of the birthday of Washington; we are met to celebrate this day. Washington is the mightiest name of earth long since mightiest in the cause of civil liberty, still mightiest in moral reformation. On that name no eulogy is expected. It cannot be. To add brightness to the sun or glory to the name of Washington is alike impossible. Let none attempt it. In solemn awe pronounce the name, and in its naked deathless splendor leave it shining on.

TO JOSHUA F. SPEED.
SPRINGFIELD, February 25, 1842.

DEAR SPEED:—Yours of the 16th instant, announcing that Miss Fanny and you are "no more twain, but one flesh," reached me this morning. I have no way of telling you how much happiness I wish you both, though I believe you both can conceive it. I feel somewhat jealous of both of you now: you will be so exclusively concerned for one another, that I shall be forgotten entirely. My acquaintance with Miss Fanny (I call her this, lest you should think I am speaking of your mother) was too short for me to reasonably hope to long be remembered by her; and still I am sure I shall not forget her soon. Try if you cannot remind her of that debt she owes me—and be sure you do not interfere to prevent her paying it.

I regret to learn that you have resolved to not return to Illinois. I shall be very lonesome without you. How miserably things seem to be arranged in this world! If we have no friends, we have no pleasure; and if we have them, we are sure to lose them, and be doubly pained by the loss. I did hope she and you would make your home here; but I own I have no right to insist. You owe obligations to her ten thousand times more sacred than you can owe to others, and in that light let them be respected and observed. It is natural that she should desire to remain with her relatives and friends. As to friends, however, she could not need them anywhere: she would have them in abundance here.

Give my kind remembrance to Mr. Williamson and his family, particularly Miss Elizabeth; also to your mother, brother, and sisters. Ask little Eliza Davis if she will ride to town with me if I come there again. And finally, give Fanny a double reciprocation of all the love she sent me. Write me often, and believe me

Yours forever, LINCOLN.

P. S. Poor Easthouse is gone at last. He died awhile before day this morning. They say he was very loath to die....

L.

TO JOSHUA F. SPEED—
ON MARRIAGE CONCERNS
SPRINGFIELD, February 25, 1842.

DEAR SPEED:—I received yours of the 12th written the day you went down to William's place, some days since, but delayed answering it till I should receive the promised one of the 16th, which came last night. I opened the letter with intense anxiety and trepidation; so much so, that, although it turned out better than I expected, I have hardly yet, at a distance of ten hours, become calm.

I tell you, Speed, our forebodings (for which you and I are peculiar) are all the worst sort of nonsense. I fancied, from the time I received your letter of Saturday, that the one of Wednesday was never to come, and yet it did come, and what is more, it is perfectly clear, both from its tone and handwriting, that you were much happier, or, if you think the term preferable, less miserable, when you wrote it than when you wrote the last one before. You had so obviously improved at the very time I so much fancied you would have grown worse. You say that something indescribably horrible and alarming still haunts you. You will not say that three months from now, I will venture. When your nerves once get steady now, the whole trouble will be over forever. Nor should you become impatient at their being even very slow in becoming steady. Again you say, you much fear that that Elysium of which you have dreamed so much is never to be realized. Well, if it shall not, I dare swear it will not be the fault of her who is now your wife. I now have no doubt that it is the peculiar misfortune of both you and me to dream dreams of Elysium far exceeding all that anything earthly can realize. Far short of your dreams as you may be, no woman could do more to realize them than that same black-eyed Fanny. If you could but contemplate her through my imagination, it would appear ridiculous to you that any one should for a moment think of being unhappy with her. My old father used to have a saying that "If you make a bad bargain, hug it all the tighter"; and it occurs to me that if the bargain you have just closed can possibly be called a bad one, it is certainly the most pleasant one for applying that maxim to which my fancy can by any effort picture.

I write another letter, enclosing this, which you can show her, if she desires it. I do this because she would think strangely, perhaps, should you tell her that you received no letters from me, or, telling her you do, refuse to let her see them. I close this, entertaining the confident hope that every successive letter I shall have from you (which I here pray may not be few, nor far between) may show you possessing a more steady hand and cheerful heart than the last preceding it. As ever, your friend, LINCOLN.

TO JOSHUA F. SPEED.
SPRINGFIELD, March 27, 1842

DEAR SPEED:—Yours of the 10th instant was received three or four days since. You know I am sincere when I tell you the pleasure its contents gave me was, and is, inexpressible. As to your farm matter, I have no sympathy with you. I have no farm, nor ever expect to have, and consequently have not studied the subject enough to be much interested with it. I can only say that I am glad you are satisfied and pleased with it. But on that other subject, to me of the most intense interest whether in joy or sorrow, I never had the power to withhold my sympathy from you. It cannot be told how it now thrills me with joy to hear you say you are "far happier than you ever expected to be." That much I know is enough. I know you too well to suppose your expectations were not, at least, sometimes extravagant, and if the reality exceeds them all, I say, Enough, dear Lord. I am not going beyond the truth when I tell you that the short space it took me to read your last letter gave me more pleasure than the total sum of all I have enjoyed since the fatal 1st of January, 1841. Since then it seems to me I should have been entirely happy, but for the never-absent idea that there is one still unhappy whom I have contributed to make so. That still kills my soul. I cannot but reproach myself for even wishing to be happy while she is otherwise. She accompanied a large party on the railroad cars to Jacksonville last Monday, and on her return spoke, so that I heard of it, of having enjoyed the trip exceedingly. God be praised for that.

You know with what sleepless vigilance I have watched you ever since the commencement of your affair; and although I am almost confident it is useless, I cannot forbear once more to say that I think it is even yet possible for your spirits to flag down and leave you miserable. If they should, don't fail to remember that they cannot long remain so. One thing I can tell you which I know you will be glad to hear, and that is that I have seen—and scrutinized her feelings as well as I could, and am fully convinced she is far happier now than she has been for the last fifteen months past.

You will see by the last Sangamon Journal, that I made a temperance speech on the 22d of February, which I claim that Fanny and you shall read as an act of charity to me; for I cannot learn that anybody else has read it, or is likely to. Fortunately it is not very long, and I shall deem it a sufficient compliance with my request if one of you listens while the other reads it.

As to your Lockridge matter, it is only necessary to say that there has been no court since you left, and that the next commences to-morrow morning, during which I suppose we cannot fail to get a judgment.

I wish you would learn of Everett what he would take, over and above a discharge for all the trouble we have been at, to take his business out of our hands and give it to somebody else. It is impossible to collect money on that or any other claim here now; and although you know I am not a very petulant man, I declare I am almost out of patience with Mr. Everett's importunity. It seems like he not only writes all the letters he can himself, but gets everybody else in Louisville and vicinity to be constantly writing to us about his claim. I have always said that Mr. Everett is a very clever fellow, and I am very sorry he cannot be obliged; but it does seem to me he ought to know we are interested to collect his claim, and therefore would do it if we could.

I am neither joking nor in a pet when I say we would thank him to transfer his business to some other, without any compensation for what we have done, provided he will see the court cost paid, for which we are security.

The sweet violet you inclosed came safely to hand, but it was so dry, and mashed so flat, that it crumbled to dust at the first attempt to handle it. The juice that mashed out of it stained a place in the letter, which I mean to preserve and cherish for the sake of her who procured it to be sent. My renewed good wishes to her in particular, and generally to all such of your relations who know me.

As ever,

LINCOLN.

TO JOSHUA F. SPEED.
SPRINGFIELD, ILLINOIS, July 4, 1842.

DEAR SPEED:—Yours of the 16th June was received only a day or two since. It was not mailed at Louisville till the 25th. You speak of the great time that has elapsed since I wrote you. Let me explain that. Your letter reached here a day or two after I started on the circuit. I was gone five or six weeks, so that I got the letters only a few weeks before Butler started to your country. I thought it scarcely worth while to write you the news which he could and would tell you more in detail. On his return he told me you would write me soon, and so I waited for your letter. As to my having been displeased with your advice, surely you know better than that. I know you do, and therefore will not labor to convince you. True, that subject is painful to me; but it is not your silence, or the silence of all the world, that can make me forget it. I acknowledge the correctness of your advice too; but before I resolve to do the one thing or the other, I must gain my confidence in my own ability to keep my resolves when they are made. In that ability you know I once prided myself as the only or chief gem of my character; that gem I lost—how and where you know too well. I have not yet regained it; and until I do, I cannot trust myself in any matter of much importance. I believe now that had you understood my case at the time as well as I understand yours afterward, by the aid you would have given me I should have sailed through clear, but that does not now afford me sufficient confidence to begin that or the like of that again.

You make a kind acknowledgment of your obligations to me for your present happiness. I am pleased with that acknowledgment. But a thousand times more am I pleased to know that you enjoy a degree of happiness worthy of an acknowledgment. The truth is, I am not sure that there was any merit with me in the part I took in your difficulty; I was drawn to it by a fate. If I would I could not have done less than I did. I always was superstitious; I believe God made me one of the instruments of bringing your Fanny and you together, which union I have no doubt He had fore-ordained. Whatever He designs He will do for me yet. "Stand still, and see the salvation of the Lord" is my text just now. If, as you say, you have told Fanny all, I should have no objection to her seeing this letter, but for its reference to our friend here: let her seeing it depend upon whether she has ever known anything of my affairs; and if she has not, do not let her.

I do not think I can come to Kentucky this season. I am so poor and make so little headway in the world, that I drop back in a month of idleness as much as I gain in a year's sowing. I should like to visit you again. I should like to see that "sis" of yours that was absent when I was there, though I suppose she would run away again if she were to hear I was coming.

My respects and esteem to all your friends there, and, by your permission, my love to your Fanny.

Ever yours,

LINCOLN.

A LETTER FROM THE LOST TOWNSHIPS

Article written by Lincoln for the Sangamon Journal in ridicule of James Shields, who, as State Auditor, had declined to receive State Bank notes in payment of taxes. The above letter purported to come from a poor widow who, though supplied with State Bank paper, could not obtain a receipt for her tax bill. This, and another subsequent letter by Mary Todd, brought about the "Lincoln-Shields Duel."

LOST TOWNSHIPS
August 27, 1842.

DEAR Mr. PRINTER:

I see you printed that long letter I sent you a spell ago. I 'm quite encouraged by it, and can't keep from writing again. I think the printing of my letters will be a good thing all round—it will give me the benefit of being known by the world, and give the world the advantage of knowing what's going on in the Lost Townships, and give your paper respectability besides. So here comes another. Yesterday afternoon I hurried through cleaning up the dinner dishes and stepped over to neighbor S——— to see if his wife Peggy was as well as mout be expected, and hear what they called the baby. Well, when I got there and just turned round the corner of his log cabin, there he was, setting on the doorstep reading a newspaper. "How are you, Jeff?" says I. He sorter started when he heard me, for he hadn't seen me before. "Why," says he, "I 'm mad as the devil, Aunt 'Becca!" "What about?" says I; "ain't its hair the right color? None of that nonsense, Jeff; there ain't an honester woman in the Lost Townships than..."—"Than who?" says he; "what the mischief are you about?" I began to see I was running the wrong trail, and so says I, "Oh! nothing: I guess I was mistaken a little, that's all. But what is it you 're mad about?"

"Why," says he, "I've been tugging ever since harvest, getting out wheat and hauling it to the river to raise State Bank paper enough to pay my tax this year and a little school debt I owe; and now, just as I 've got it, here I open this infernal Extra Register, expecting to find it full of 'Glorious Democratic Victories' and 'High Comb'd Cocks,' when, lo and behold! I find a set of fellows, calling themselves officers of the State, have forbidden the tax collectors, and school commissioners to receive State paper at all; and so here it is dead on my hands. I don't now believe all the plunder I've got will fetch ready cash enough to pay my taxes and that school debt."

I was a good deal thunderstruck myself; for that was the first I had heard of the proclamation, and my old man was pretty much in the same fix with Jeff. We both stood a moment staring at one another without knowing what to say. At last says I, "Mr. S——— let me look at that paper." He handed it to me, when I read the proclamation over.

"There now," says he, "did you ever see such a piece of impudence and imposition as that?" I saw Jeff was in a good tune for saying some ill-natured things, and so I tho't I would just argue a little on the contrary side, and make him rant a spell if I could. "Why," says I, looking as dignified and thoughtful as I could, "it seems pretty tough, to be sure, to have to raise silver where there's none to be raised; but then, you see, 'there will be danger of loss' if it ain't done."

"Loss! damnation!" says he. "I defy Daniel Webster, I defy King Solomon, I defy the world—I defy—I defy—yes, I defy even you, Aunt 'Becca, to show how the people can lose anything by paying their taxes in State paper."

"Well," says I, "you see what the officers of State say about it, and they are a desarnin' set of men. But," says I, "I guess you 're mistaken about what the proclamation says. It don't say the people will lose anything by the paper money being taken for taxes. It only says 'there will be danger of loss'; and though it is tolerable plain that the people can't lose by paying their taxes in something they can get easier than silver, instead of having to pay silver; and though it's just as plain that the State can't lose by taking State Bank paper, however low it may be, while she owes the bank more than the whole revenue, and can pay that paper over on her debt, dollar for dollar;—still there is danger of loss to the 'officers of State'; and you know, Jeff, we can't get along without officers of State."

"Damn officers of State!" says he; "that's what Whigs are always hurrahing for."

"Now, don't swear so, Jeff," says I, "you know I belong to the meetin', and swearin' hurts my feelings."

"Beg pardon, Aunt 'Becca," says he; "but I do say it's enough to make Dr. Goddard swear, to have tax to pay in silver, for nothing only that Ford may get his two thousand a year, and Shields his twenty-four hundred a year, and Carpenter his sixteen hundred a year, and all without 'danger of loss' by taking it in State paper. Yes, yes: it's plain enough now what these officers of State mean by 'danger of loss.' Wash, I s'pose, actually lost fifteen hundred dollars out of the three thousand that two of these 'officers of State' let him steal from the treasury, by being compelled to take it in State paper. Wonder if we don't have a proclamation before long, commanding us to make up this loss to Wash in silver."

And so he went on till his breath run out, and he had to stop. I couldn't think of anything to say just then, and so I begun to look over the paper again. "Ay! here's another proclamation, or something like it."

"Another?" says Jeff; "and whose egg is it, pray?"

I looked to the bottom of it, and read aloud, "Your obedient servant, James Shields, Auditor."

"Aha!" says Jeff, "one of them same three fellows again. Well read it, and let's hear what of it."

I read on till I came to where it says, "The object of this measure is to suspend the collection of the revenue for the current year."

"Now stop, now stop!" says he; "that's a lie a'ready, and I don't want to hear of it."

"Oh, maybe not," says I.

"I say it-is-a-lie. Suspend the collection, indeed! Will the collectors, that have taken their oaths to make the collection, dare to end it? Is there anything in law requiring them to perjure themselves at the bidding of James Shields?

"Will the greedy gullet of the penitentiary be satisfied with swallowing him instead of all of them, if they should venture to obey him? And would he not discover some 'danger of loss,' and be off about the time it came to taking their places?

"And suppose the people attempt to suspend, by refusing to pay; what then? The collectors would just jerk up their horses and cows, and the like, and sell them to the highest bidder for silver in hand, without valuation or redemption. Why, Shields didn't believe that story himself; it was never meant for the truth. If it was true, why was it not writ till five days after the proclamation? Why did n't Carlin and Carpenter sign it as well as Shields? Answer me that, Aunt 'Becca. I say it's a lie, and not a well told one at that. It grins out like a copper dollar. Shields is a fool as well as a liar. With him truth is out of the question; and as for getting a good, bright, passable lie out of him, you might as well try to strike fire from a cake of tallow. I stick to it, it's all an infernal Whig lie!"

"A Whig lie! Highty tighty!"

"Yes, a Whig lie; and it's just like everything the cursed British Whigs do. First they'll do some divilment, and then they'll tell a lie to hide it. And they don't care how plain a lie it is; they think they can cram any sort of a one down the throats of the ignorant Locofocos, as they call the Democrats."

"Why, Jeff, you 're crazy: you don't mean to say Shields is a Whig!"

"Yes, I do."

"Why, look here! the proclamation is in your own Democratic paper, as you call it."

"I know it; and what of that? They only printed it to let us Democrats see the deviltry the Whigs are at."

"Well, but Shields is the auditor of this Loco—I mean this Democratic State."

"So he is, and Tyler appointed him to office."

"Tyler appointed him?"

"Yes (if you must chaw it over), Tyler appointed him; or, if it was n't him, it was old Granny Harrison, and that's all one. I tell you, Aunt 'Becca, there's no mistake about his being a Whig. Why, his very looks shows it; everything about him shows it: if I was deaf and blind, I could tell him by the smell. I seed him when I was down in Springfield last winter. They had a sort of a gatherin' there one night among the grandees, they called a fair. All the gals about town was there, and all the handsome widows and married women, finickin' about trying to look like gals, tied as tight in the middle, and puffed out at both ends, like bundles of fodder that had n't been stacked yet, but wanted stackin' pretty bad. And then they had tables all around the house kivered over with [———] caps and pincushions and ten thousand such little knick-knacks, tryin' to sell 'em to the fellows that were bowin', and scrapin' and kungeerin' about 'em. They would n't let no Democrats in, for fear they'd disgust the ladies, or scare the little gals, or dirty the floor. I looked in at the window, and there was this same fellow Shields floatin' about on the air, without heft or earthly substances, just like a lock of cat fur where cats had been fighting.

"He was paying his money to this one, and that one, and t' other one, and sufferin' great loss because it was n't silver instead of State paper; and the sweet distress he seemed to be in,—his very features, in the ecstatic agony of his soul, spoke audibly and distinctly, 'Dear girls, it is distressing, but I cannot marry you all. Too well I know how much you suffer; but do, do remember, it is not my fault that I am so handsome and so interesting.'

"As this last was expressed by a most exquisite contortion of his face, he seized hold of one of their hands, and squeezed, and held on to it about a quarter of an hour. 'Oh, my good fellow!' says I to myself, 'if that was one of our Democratic gals in the Lost Townships, the way you 'd get a brass pin let into you would be about up to the head.' He a Democrat! Fiddlesticks! I tell you, Aunt 'Becca, he's a Whig, and no mistake; nobody but a Whig could make such a conceity dunce of himself."

"Well," says I, "maybe he is; but, if he is, I 'm mistaken the worst sort. Maybe so, maybe so; but, if I am, I'll suffer by it; I'll be a Democrat if it turns out that Shields is a Whig, considerin' you shall be a Whig if he turns out a Democrat."

"A bargain, by jingoes!" says he; "but how will we find out?"

"Why," says I, "we'll just write and ax the printer."

"Agreed again!" says he; "and by thunder! if it does turn out that Shields is a Democrat, I never will——"

"Jefferson! Jefferson!"

"What do you want, Peggy?"

170

"Do get through your everlasting clatter some time, and bring me a gourd of water; the child's been crying for a drink this livelong hour."

"Let it die, then; it may as well die for water as to be taxed to death to fatten officers of State."

Jeff run off to get the water, though, just like he hadn't been saying anything spiteful, for he's a raal good-hearted fellow, after all, once you get at the foundation of him.

I walked into the house, and, "Why, Peggy," says I, "I declare we like to forgot you altogether."

"Oh, yes," says she, "when a body can't help themselves, everybody soon forgets 'em; but, thank God! by day after to-morrow I shall be well enough to milk the cows, and pen the calves, and wring the contrary ones' tails for 'em, and no thanks to nobody."

"Good evening, Peggy," says I, and so I sloped, for I seed she was mad at me for making Jeff neglect her so long.

And now, Mr. Printer, will you be sure to let us know in your next paper whether this Shields is a Whig or a Democrat? I don't care about it for myself, for I know well enough how it is already; but I want to convince Jeff. It may do some good to let him, and others like him, know who and what these officers of State are. It may help to send the present hypocritical set to where they belong, and to fill the places they now disgrace with men who will do more work for less pay, and take fewer airs while they are doing it. It ain't sensible to think that the same men who get us in trouble will change their course; and yet it's pretty plain if some change for the better is not made, it's not long that either Peggy or I or any of us will have a cow left to milk, or a calf's tail to wring.

Yours truly,

REBECCA ———.

INVITATION TO HENRY CLAY.
SPRINGFIELD, ILL., Aug 29, 1842.

HON. HENRY CLAY, Lexington, Ky.

DEAR SIR:—We hear you are to visit Indianapolis, Indiana, on the 5th Of October next. If our information in this is correct we hope you will not deny us the pleasure of seeing you in our State. We are aware of the toil necessarily incident to a journey by one circumstanced as you are; but once you have embarked, as you have already determined to do, the toil would not be greatly augmented by extending the journey to our capital. The season of the year will be most favorable for good roads, and pleasant weather; and although we cannot but believe you would be highly gratified with such a visit to the prairie-land, the pleasure it would give us and thousands such as we is beyond all question. You have never visited Illinois, or at least this portion of it; and should you now yield to our request, we promise you such a reception as shall be worthy of the man on whom are now turned the fondest hopes of a great and suffering nation.

Please inform us at the earliest convenience whether we may expect you.

Very respectfully your obedient servants,
A. G. HENRY, A. T. BLEDSOE,
C. BIRCHALL, A. LINCOLN,
G. M. CABANNISS, ROB'T IRWIN,
P. A. SAUNDERS, J. M. ALLEN,
F. N. FRANCIS.
Executive Committee "Clay Club."
(Clay's answer, September 6, 1842, declines with thanks.)

CORRESPONDENCE ABOUT THE LINCOLN-SHIELDS DUEL. TREMONT, September 17, 1842.

ABRA. LINCOLN, ESQ.:—I regret that my absence on public business compelled me to postpone a matter of private consideration a little longer than I could have desired. It will only be necessary, however, to account for it by informing you that I have been to Quincy on business that would not admit of delay. I will now state briefly the reasons of my troubling you with this communication, the disagreeable nature of which I regret, as I had hoped to avoid any difficulty with any one in Springfield while residing there, by endeavoring to conduct myself in such a way amongst both my political friends and opponents as to escape the necessity of any. Whilst thus abstaining from giving provocation, I have become the object of slander, vituperation, and personal abuse, which were I capable of submitting to, I would prove myself worthy of the whole of it.

In two or three of the last numbers of the Sangamon Journal, articles of the most personal nature and calculated to degrade me have made their appearance. On inquiring, I was informed by the editor of that paper, through the medium of my friend General Whitesides, that you are the author of those articles. This information satisfies me that I have become by some means or other the object of your secret hostility. I will not take the trouble of inquiring into the reason of all this; but I will take the liberty of requiring a full, positive, and absolute retraction of all offensive allusions used by you in these communications, in relation to my private character and standing as a man, as an apology for the insults conveyed in them.

This may prevent consequences which no one will regret more than myself.

Your obedient servant, JAS. SHIELDS.

TO J. SHIELDS.
TREMONT, September 17, 1842

JAS. SHIELDS, ESQ.:—Your note of to-day was handed me by General Whitesides. In that note you say you have been informed, through the medium of the editor of the Journal, that I am the author of certain articles in that paper which you deem personally abusive of you; and without stopping to inquire whether I really am the author, or to point out what is offensive in them, you demand an unqualified retraction of all that is offensive, and then proceed to hint at consequences.

Now, sir, there is in this so much assumption of facts and so much of menace as to consequences, that I cannot submit to answer that note any further than I have, and to add that the consequences to which I suppose you allude would be matter of as great regret to me as it possibly could to you.

Respectfully,

A. LINCOLN.

TO A. LINCOLN FROM JAS. SHIELDS
TREMONT, September 17, 1842.

ABRA. LINCOLN, ESQ.:—In reply to my note of this date, you intimate that I assume facts and menace consequences, and that you cannot submit to answer it further. As now, sir, you desire it, I will be a little more particular. The editor of the Sangamon Journal gave me to understand that you are the author of an article which appeared, I think, in that paper of the 2d September instant, headed "The Lost Townships," and signed Rebecca or 'Becca. I would therefore take the liberty of asking whether you are the author of said article, or any other over the same signature which has appeared in any of the late numbers of that paper. If so, I repeat my request of an absolute retraction of all offensive allusions contained therein in relation to my private character and standing. If you are not the author of any of these articles, your denial will be sufficient. I will say further, it is not my intention to menace, but to do myself justice.

Your obedient servant, JAS. SHIELDS.

MEMORANDUM OF INSTRUCTIONS
TO E. H. MERRYMAN,
Lincoln's Second,
September 19, 1842.

In case Whitesides shall signify a wish to adjust this affair without further difficulty, let him know that if the present papers be withdrawn, and a note from Mr. Shields asking to know if I am the author of the articles of which he complains, and asking that I shall make him gentlemanly satisfaction if I am the author, and this without menace, or dictation as to what that satisfaction shall be, a pledge is made that the following answer shall be given:

"I did write the 'Lost Townships' letter which appeared in the Journal of the 2d instant, but had no participation in any form in any other article alluding to you. I wrote that wholly for political effect—I had no intention of injuring your personal or private character or standing as a man or a gentleman; and I did not then think, and do not now think, that that article could produce or has produced that effect against you; and had I anticipated such an effect I would have forborne to write it. And I will add that your conduct toward me, so far as I know, had always been gentlemanly; and that I had no personal pique against you, and no cause for any."

If this should be done, I leave it with you to arrange what shall and what shall not be published. If nothing like this is done, the preliminaries of the fight are to be—

First. Weapons: Cavalry broadswords of the largest size, precisely equal in all respects, and such as now used by the cavalry company at Jacksonville.

Second. Position: A plank ten feet long, and from nine to twelve inches broad, to be firmly fixed on edge, on the ground, as the line between us, which neither is to pass his foot over upon forfeit of his life. Next a line drawn on the ground on either side of said plank and parallel with it, each at the distance of the whole length of the sword and three feet additional from the plank; and the passing of his own such line by either party during the fight shall be deemed a surrender of the contest.

Third. Time: On Thursday evening at five o'clock, if you can get it so; but in no case to be at a greater distance of time than Friday evening at five o'clock.

Fourth. Place: Within three miles of Alton, on the opposite side of the river, the particular spot to be agreed on by you.

Any preliminary details coming within the above rules you are at liberty to make at your discretion; but you are in no case to swerve from these rules, or to pass beyond their limits.

TO JOSHUA F. SPEED.
SPRINGFIELD, October 4, 1842.

DEAR SPEED:—You have heard of my duel with Shields, and I have now to inform you that the dueling business still rages in this city. Day before yesterday Shields challenged Butler, who accepted, and proposed fighting next morning at sunrise in Bob Allen's meadow, one hundred yards' distance, with rifles. To this Whitesides, Shields's second, said "No," because of the law. Thus ended duel No. 2.

175

Yesterday Whitesides chose to consider himself insulted by Dr. Merryman, so sent him a kind of quasi-challenge, inviting him to meet him at the Planter's House in St. Louis on the next Friday, to settle their difficulty. Merryman made me his friend, and sent Whitesides a note, inquiring to know if he meant his note as a challenge, and if so, that he would, according to the law in such case made and provided, prescribe the terms of the meeting. Whitesides returned for answer that if Merryman would meet him at the Planter's House as desired, he would challenge him. Merryman replied in a note that he denied Whitesides's right to dictate time and place, but that he (Merryman) would waive the question of time, and meet him at Louisiana, Missouri. Upon my presenting this note to Whitesides and stating verbally its contents, he declined receiving it, saying he had business in St. Louis, and it was as near as Louisiana. Merryman then directed me to notify Whitesides that he should publish the correspondence between them, with such comments as he thought fit. This I did. Thus it stood at bedtime last night. This morning Whitesides, by his friend Shields, is praying for a new trial, on the ground that he was mistaken in Merryman's proposition to meet him at Louisiana, Missouri, thinking it was the State of Louisiana. This Merryman hoots at, and is preparing his publication; while the town is in a ferment, and a street fight somewhat anticipated.

But I began this letter not for what I have been writing, but to say something on that subject which you know to be of such infinite solicitude to me. The immense sufferings you endured from the first days of September till the middle of February you never tried to conceal from me, and I well understood. You have now been the husband of a lovely woman nearly eight months. That you are happier now than the day you married her I well know, for without you could not be living. But I have your word for it, too, and the returning elasticity of spirits which is manifested in your letters. But I want to ask a close question, "Are you now in feeling as well as judgment glad that you are married as you are?" From anybody but me this would be an impudent question, not to be tolerated; but I know you will pardon it in me. Please answer it quickly, as I am impatient to know. I have sent my love to your Fanny so often, I fear she is getting tired of it. However, I venture to tender it again.

Yours forever,

LINCOLN.

176

TO JAMES S. IRWIN.
SPRINGFIELD, November 2, 1842.
JAS. S. IRWIN ESQ.:

Owing to my absence, yours of the 22nd ult. was not received till this moment. Judge Logan and myself are willing to attend to any business in the Supreme Court you may send us. As to fees, it is impossible to establish a rule that will apply in all, or even a great many cases. We believe we are never accused of being very unreasonable in this particular; and we would always be easily satisfied, provided we could see the money—but whatever fees we earn at a distance, if not paid before, we have noticed, we never hear of after the work is done. We, therefore, are growing a little sensitive on that point.

Yours etc.,

A. LINCOLN.

1843

RESOLUTIONS AT A WHIG MEETING AT SPRINGFIELD, ILLINOIS, MARCH 1, 1843.

The object of the meeting was stated by Mr. Lincoln of Springfield, who offered the following resolutions, which were unanimously adopted:

Resolved, That a tariff of duties on imported goods, producing sufficient revenue for the payment of the necessary expenditures of the National Government, and so adjusted as to protect American industry, is indispensably necessary to the prosperity of the American people.

Resolved, That we are opposed to direct taxation for the support of the National Government.

Resolved, That a national bank, properly restricted, is highly necessary and proper to the establishment and maintenance of a sound

177

currency, and for the cheap and safe collection, keeping, and disbursing of the public revenue.

Resolved, That the distribution of the proceeds of the sales of the public lands, upon the principles of Mr. Clay's bill, accords with the best interests of the nation, and particularly with those of the State of Illinois.

Resolved, That we recommend to the Whigs of each Congressional district of the State to nominate and support at the approaching election a candidate of their own principles, regardless of the chances of success.

Resolved, That we recommend to the Whigs of all portions of the State to adopt and rigidly adhere to the convention system of nominating candidates.

Resolved, That we recommend to the Whigs of each Congressional district to hold a district convention on or before the first Monday of May next, to be composed of a number of delegates from each county equal to double the number of its representatives in the General Assembly, provided, each county shall have at least one delegate. Said delegates to be chosen by primary meetings of the Whigs, at such times and places as they in their respective counties may see fit. Said district conventions each to nominate one candidate for Congress, and one delegate to a national convention for the purpose of nominating candidates for President and Vice-President of the United States. The seven delegates so nominated to a national convention to have power to add two delegates to their own number, and to fill all vacancies.

Resolved, That A. T. Bledsoe, S. T. Logan, and A. Lincoln be appointed a committee to prepare an address to the people of the State.

Resolved, That N. W. Edwards, A. G. Henry, James H. Matheny, John C. Doremus, and James C. Conkling be appointed a Whig Central State Committee, with authority to fill any vacancy that may occur in the committee.

CIRCULAR FROM WHIG COMMITTEE.
Address to the People of Illinois.

FELLOW-CITIZENS:-By a resolution of a meeting of such of the Whigs of the State as are now at Springfield, we, the undersigned, were appointed to prepare an address to you. The performance of that task we now undertake.

Several resolutions were adopted by the meeting; and the chief object of this address is to show briefly the reasons for their adoption.

The first of those resolutions declares a tariff of duties upon foreign importations, producing sufficient revenue for the support of the General Government, and so adjusted as to protect American industry, to be indispensably necessary to the prosperity of the American people; and the second declares direct taxation for a national revenue to be improper. Those two resolutions are kindred in their nature, and therefore proper and convenient to be considered together. The question of protection is a subject entirely too broad to be crowded into a few pages only, together with several other subjects. On that point we therefore content ourselves with giving the following extracts from the writings of Mr. Jefferson, General Jackson, and the speech of Mr. Calhoun:

"To be independent for the comforts of life, we must fabricate them ourselves. We must now place the manufacturer by the side of the agriculturalist. The grand inquiry now is, Shall we make our own comforts, or go without them at the will of a foreign nation? He, therefore, who is now against domestic manufactures must be for reducing us either to dependence on that foreign nation, or to be clothed in skins and to live like wild beasts in dens and caverns. I am not one of those; experience has taught me that manufactures are now as necessary to our independence as to our comfort." Letter of Mr. Jefferson to Benjamin Austin.

"I ask, What is the real situation of the agriculturalist? Where has the American farmer a market for his surplus produce? Except for cotton, he has neither a foreign nor a home market. Does not this clearly prove, when there is no market at home or abroad, that there [is] too much labor employed in agriculture? Common sense at once points out the remedy. Take from agriculture six hundred thousand men, women, and children, and you will at once give a market for more breadstuffs than all Europe now furnishes. In short, we have been too long subject to the policy of British merchants. It is time we should become a little more Americanized, and instead of feeding the paupers and laborers of England, feed our own; or else in a short time, by continuing our present policy, we shall all be rendered paupers ourselves."—General Jackson's Letter to Dr. Coleman.

"When our manufactures are grown to a certain perfection, as they soon will be, under the fostering care of government, the farmer will find a ready market for his surplus produce, and—what is of equal consequence—a certain and cheap supply of all he wants; his prosperity will diffuse itself to every class of the community." Speech of Hon. J. C. Calhoun on the Tariff.

The question of revenue we will now briefly consider. For several years past the revenues of the government have been unequal to its expenditures, and consequently loan after loan, sometimes direct and sometimes indirect in form, has been resorted to. By this means a new national debt has been created, and is still growing on us with a rapidity fearful to contemplate—a rapidity only reasonably to be expected in time of war. This state of things has been produced by a prevailing unwillingness either to increase the tariff or resort to direct taxation. But the one or the other must come. Coming expenditures must be met, and the present debt must be paid; and money cannot always be borrowed for these objects. The system of loans is but temporary in its nature, and must soon explode. It is a system not only ruinous while it lasts, but one that must soon fail and leave us destitute. As an individual who undertakes to live by borrowing soon finds his original means devoured by interest, and, next, no one left to borrow from, so must it be with a government.

We repeat, then, that a tariff sufficient for revenue, or a direct tax, must soon be resorted to; and, indeed, we believe this alternative is now denied by no one. But which system shall be adopted? Some of our opponents, in theory, admit the propriety of a tariff sufficient for a revenue, but even they will not in practice vote for such a tariff; while others boldly advocate direct taxation. Inasmuch, therefore, as some of them boldly advocate direct taxation, and all the rest—or so nearly all as to make exceptions needless—refuse to adopt the tariff, we think it is doing them no injustice to class them all as advocates of direct taxation. Indeed, we believe they are only delaying an open avowal of the system till they can assure themselves that the people will tolerate it. Let us, then, briefly compare the two systems. The tariff is the cheaper system, because the duties, being collected in large parcels at a few commercial points, will require comparatively few officers in their collection; while by the direct-tax system the land must be literally covered with assessors and collectors, going forth like swarms of Egyptian locusts, devouring every blade of grass and other green thing. And, again, by the tariff system the whole revenue is paid by the consumers of foreign goods, and those chiefly the luxuries, and not the necessaries, of life. By this system the man who contents himself to live upon the products of his own country pays nothing at all. And surely that country is extensive enough, and its products abundant and varied enough, to answer all the real wants of its people. In short, by this system the burthen of revenue falls almost entirely on the wealthy and luxurious few, while the substantial and laboring many who live at home, and upon home products, go entirely free. By the direct-tax system none can escape. However strictly the citizen may exclude from his premises all foreign luxuries,—fine cloths, fine silks, rich wines, golden chains, and diamond rings,—still, for the possession of his house, his barn, and his homespun, he is to be perpetually haunted and harassed by the tax-gatherer. With these views we leave it to be determined whether we or our opponents are the more truly democratic on the subject.

The third resolution declares the necessity and propriety of a national bank. During the last fifty years so much has been said and written both as to the constitutionality and expediency of such an institution, that we could not hope to improve in the least on former discussions of the subject, were we to undertake it. We, therefore, upon the question of constitutionality content ourselves with remarking the facts that the first national bank was established chiefly by the same men who formed the Constitution, at a time when that instrument was but two years old, and receiving the sanction, as President, of the immortal Washington; that the second received the sanction, as President, of Mr. Madison, to whom common consent has awarded the proud title of "Father of the Constitution"; and subsequently the sanction of the Supreme Court, the most enlightened judicial tribunal in the world. Upon the question of expediency, we only ask you to examine the history of the times during the existence of the two banks, and compare those times with the miserable present.

The fourth resolution declares the expediency of Mr. Clay's land bill. Much incomprehensible jargon is often used against the constitutionality of this measure. We forbear, in this place, attempting an answer to it, simply because, in our opinion, those who urge it are through party zeal resolved not to see or acknowledge the truth. The question of expediency, at least so far as Illinois is concerned, seems to us the clearest imaginable. By the bill we are to receive annually a large sum of money, no part of which we otherwise receive. The precise annual sum cannot be known in advance; it doubtless will vary in different years. Still it is something to know that in the last year—a year of almost unparalleled pecuniary pressure—it amounted to more than forty thousand dollars. This annual income, in the midst of our almost insupportable difficulties, in the days of our severest necessity, our political opponents are furiously resolving to take and keep from us. And for what? Many silly reasons are given, as is usual in cases where a single good one is not to be found. One is that by giving us the proceeds of the lands we impoverish the national treasury, and thereby render necessary an increase of the tariff. This may be true; but if so, the amount of it only is that those whose pride, whose abundance of means, prompt them to spurn the manufactures of our country, and to strut in British cloaks and coats and pantaloons, may have to pay a few cents more on the yard for the cloth that makes them. A terrible evil, truly, to the Illinois farmer, who never wore, nor ever expects to wear, a single yard of British goods in his whole life. Another of their reasons is that by the passage and continuance of Mr. Clay's bill, we prevent the passage of a bill which would give us more. This, if it were sound in itself, is waging destructive war with the former position; for if Mr. Clay's bill impoverishes the treasury too much, what shall be said of one that impoverishes it still more? But it is not sound in itself. It is not true that Mr. Clay's bill prevents the passage of one more favorable to us of the new States. Considering the strength and opposite interest of the old States, the wonder is that they ever permitted one to pass so favorable as Mr. Clay's. The last twenty-odd years' efforts to reduce the price of the lands, and to pass graduation bills and cession bills, prove the assertion to be true; and if there were no experience in support of it, the reason itself is plain. The States in which none, or few, of the public lands lie, and those consequently interested against parting with them except for the best price, are the majority; and a moment's reflection will show that they must ever continue the majority, because by the time one of the original new States (Ohio, for example) becomes populous and gets weight in Congress, the public lands in her limits are so nearly sold out that in every point material to this question she becomes an old State. She does not wish the price reduced, because there is none left for her citizens to buy; she does not wish them ceded to the States in which they lie, because they no longer lie in her limits, and she will get nothing by the cession. In the nature of things, the States interested in the reduction of price, in graduation, in cession, and in all similar projects, never can be the majority. Nor is there reason to hope that any of them can ever succeed as a Democratic party measure, because we have heretofore seen that party in full power, year after year, with many of their leaders making loud professions in favor of these projects, and yet doing nothing. What reason, then, is there to believe they will hereafter do better? In every light in which we can view this question, it amounts simply to this: Shall we accept our share of the proceeds under Mr. Clay's bill, or shall we rather reject that and get nothing?

The fifth resolution recommends that a Whig candidate for Congress be run in every district, regardless of the chances of success. We are aware that it is sometimes a temporary gratification, when a friend cannot succeed, to be able to choose between opponents; but we believe that that gratification is the seed-time which never fails to be followed by a most abundant harvest of bitterness. By this policy we entangle ourselves. By voting for our opponents, such of us as do it in some measure estop ourselves to complain of their acts, however glaringly wrong we may believe them to be. By this policy no one portion of our friends can ever be certain as to what course another portion may adopt; and by this want of mutual and perfect understanding our political identity is partially frittered away and lost. And, again, those who are thus elected by our aid ever become our bitterest persecutors. Take a few prominent examples. In 1830 Reynolds was elected Governor; in 1835 we exerted our whole strength to elect Judge Young to the United States Senate, which effort, though failing, gave him the prominence that subsequently elected him; in 1836 General Ewing, was so elected to the United States Senate; and yet let us ask what three men have been more perseveringly vindictive in their assaults upon all our men and measures than they? During the last summer the whole State was covered with pamphlet editions of misrepresentations against us, methodized into chapters and verses, written by two of these same men,—Reynolds and Young, in which they did not stop at charging us with error merely, but roundly denounced us as the designing enemies of human liberty, itself. If it be the will of Heaven that such men shall politically live, be it so; but never, never again permit them to draw a particle of their sustenance from us.

The sixth resolution recommends the adoption of the convention system for the nomination of candidates. This we believe to be of the very first importance. Whether the system is right in itself we do not stop to inquire; contenting ourselves with trying to show that, while our opponents use it, it is madness in us not to defend ourselves with it. Experience has shown that we cannot successfully defend ourselves without it. For examples, look at the elections of last year. Our candidate for governor, with the approbation of a large portion of the party, took the field without a nomination, and in open opposition to the system. Wherever in the counties the Whigs had held conventions and nominated candidates for the Legislature, the aspirants who were not nominated were induced to rebel against the nominations, and to become candidates, as is said, "on their own hook." And, go where you would into a large Whig county, you were sure to find the Whigs not contending shoulder to shoulder against the common enemy, but divided into factions, and fighting furiously with one another. The election came, and what was the result? The governor beaten, the Whig vote being decreased many thousands since 1840, although the Democratic vote had not increased any. Beaten almost everywhere for members of the Legislature,—Tazewell, with her four hundred Whig majority, sending a delegation half Democratic; Vermillion, with her five hundred, doing the same; Coles, with her four hundred, sending two out of three; and Morgan, with her two hundred and fifty, sending three out of four,—and this to say nothing of the numerous other less glaring examples; the whole winding up with the aggregate number of twenty-seven Democratic representatives sent from Whig counties. As to the senators, too, the result was of the same character. And it is most worthy to be remembered that of all the Whigs in the State who ran against the regular nominees, a single one only was elected. Although they succeeded in defeating the nominees almost by scores, they too were defeated, and the spoils chucklingly borne off by the common enemy.

We do not mention the fact of many of the Whigs opposing the convention system heretofore for the purpose of censuring them. Far from it. We expressly protest against such a conclusion. We know they were generally, perhaps universally, as good and true Whigs as we ourselves claim to be.

We mention it merely to draw attention to the disastrous result it produced, as an example forever hereafter to be avoided. That "union is strength" is a truth that has been known, illustrated, and declared in various ways and forms in all ages of the world. That great fabulist and philosopher Aesop illustrated it by his fable of the bundle of sticks; and he whose wisdom surpasses that of all philosophers has declared that "a house divided against itself cannot stand." It is to induce our friends to act upon this important and universally acknowledged truth that we urge the adoption of the convention system. Reflection will prove that there is no other way of practically applying it. In its application we know there will be incidents temporarily painful; but, after all, those incidents will be fewer and less intense with than without the system. If two friends aspire to the same office it is certain that both cannot succeed. Would it not, then, be much less painful to have the question decided by mutual friends some time before, than to snarl and quarrel until the day of election, and then both be beaten by the common enemy?

Before leaving this subject, we think proper to remark that we do not understand the resolution as intended to recommend the application of the convention system to the nomination of candidates for the small offices no way connected with politics; though we must say we do not perceive that such an application of it would be wrong.

The seventh resolution recommends the holding of district conventions in May next, for the purpose of nominating candidates for Congress. The propriety of this rests upon the same reasons with that of the sixth, and therefore needs no further discussion.

The eighth and ninth also relate merely to the practical application of the foregoing, and therefore need no discussion.

Before closing, permit us to add a few reflections on the present condition and future prospects of the Whig party. In almost all the States we have fallen into the minority, and despondency seems to prevail universally among us. Is there just cause for this? In 1840 we carried the nation by more than a hundred and forty thousand majority. Our opponents charged that we did it by fraudulent voting; but whatever they may have believed, we know the charge to be untrue. Where, now, is that mighty host? Have they gone over to the enemy? Let the results of the late elections answer. Every State which has fallen off from the Whig cause since 1840 has done so not by giving more Democratic votes than they did then, but by giving fewer Whig. Bouck, who was elected Democratic Governor of New York last fall by more than 15,000 majority, had not then as many votes as he had in 1840, when he was beaten by seven or eight thousand. And so has it been in all the other States which have fallen away from our cause. From this it is evident that tens of thousands in the late elections have not voted at all. Who and what are they? is an important question, as respects the future. They can come forward and give us the victory again. That all, or nearly all, of them are Whigs is most apparent. Our opponents, stung to madness by the defeat of 1840, have ever since rallied with more than their usual unanimity. It has not been they that have been kept from the polls. These facts show what the result must be, once the people again rally in their entire strength. Proclaim these facts, and predict this result; and although unthinking opponents may smile at us, the sagacious ones will "believe and tremble." And why shall the Whigs not all rally again? Are their principles less dear now than in 1840? Have any of their doctrines since then been discovered to be untrue? It is true, the victory of 1840 did not produce the happy results anticipated; but it is equally true, as we believe, that the unfortunate death of General Harrison was the cause of the failure. It was not the election of General Harrison that was expected to produce happy effects, but the measures to be adopted by his administration. By means of his death, and the unexpected course of his successor, those measures were never adopted. How could the fruits follow? The consequences we always predicted would follow the failure of those measures have followed, and are now upon us in all their horrors. By the course of Mr. Tyler the policy of our opponents has continued in operation, still leaving them with the advantage of charging all its evils upon us as the results of a Whig administration. Let none be deceived by this somewhat plausible, though entirely false charge. If they ask us for the sufficient and sound currency we promised, let them be answered that we only promised it through the medium of a national bank, which they, aided by Mr. Tyler, prevented our establishing. And let them be reminded, too, that their own policy in relation to the currency has all the time been, and still is, in full operation. Let us then again come forth in our might, and by a second victory accomplish that which death prevented in the first. We can do it. When did the Whigs ever fail if they were fully aroused and united? Even in single States, under such circumstances, defeat seldom overtakes them. Call to mind the contested elections within the last few years, and particularly those of Moore and Letcher from Kentucky, Newland and Graham from North Carolina, and the famous New Jersey case. In all these districts Locofocoism had stalked omnipotent before; but when the whole people were aroused by its enormities on those occasions, they put it down, never to rise again.

We declare it to be our solemn conviction, that the Whigs are always a majority of this nation; and that to make them always successful needs but to get them all to the polls and to vote unitedly. This is the great desideratum. Let us make every effort to attain it. At every election, let every Whig act as though he knew the result to depend upon his action. In the great contest of 1840 some more than twenty one hundred thousand votes were cast, and so surely as there shall be that many, with the ordinary increase added, cast in 1844 that surely will a Whig be elected President of the United States.

A. LINCOLN. S. T. LOGAN. A. T. BLEDSOE.
March 4, 1843.

TO JOHN BENNETT.
SPRINGFIELD, March 7, 1843.
FRIEND BENNETT:

Your letter of this day was handed me by Mr. Miles. It is too late now to effect the object you desire. On yesterday morning the most of the Whig members from this district got together and agreed to hold the convention at Tremont in Tazewell County. I am sorry to hear that any of the Whigs of your county, or indeed of any county, should longer be against conventions. On last Wednesday evening a meeting of all the Whigs then here from all parts of the State was held, and the question of the propriety of conventions was brought up and fully discussed, and at the end of the discussion a resolution recommending the system of conventions to all the Whigs of the State was unanimously adopted. Other resolutions were also passed, all of which will appear in the next Journal. The meeting also appointed a committee to draft an address to the people of the State, which address will also appear in the next journal.

In it you will find a brief argument in favor of conventions—and although I wrote it myself I will say to you that it is conclusive upon the point and can not be reasonably answered. The right way for you to do is hold your meeting and appoint delegates any how, and if there be any who will not take part, let it be so. The matter will work so well this time that even they who now oppose will come in next time.

The convention is to be held at Tremont on the 5th of April and according to the rule we have adopted your county is to have delegates—being double your representation.

If there be any good Whig who is disposed to stick out against conventions get him at least to read the arguement in their favor in the address.

Yours as ever,

A. LINCOLN.

JOSHUA F. SPEED.
SPRINGFIELD, March 24, 1843.

DEAR SPEED:—We had a meeting of the Whigs of the county here on last Monday to appoint delegates to a district convention; and Baker beat me, and got the delegation instructed to go for him. The meeting, in spite of my attempt to decline it, appointed me one of the delegates; so that in getting Baker the nomination I shall be fixed a good deal like a fellow who is made a groomsman to a man that has cut him out and is marrying his own dear "gal." About the prospects of your having a namesake at our town, can't say exactly yet.

A. LINCOLN.

TO MARTIN M. MORRIS.
SPRINGFIELD, ILL., March 26, 1843.
FRIEND MORRIS:

Your letter of the a 3 d, was received on yesterday morning, and for which (instead of an excuse, which you thought proper to ask) I tender you my sincere thanks. It is truly gratifying to me to learn that, while the people of Sangamon have cast me off, my old friends of Menard, who have known me longest and best, stick to me. It would astonish, if not amuse, the older citizens to learn that I (a stranger, friendless, uneducated, penniless boy, working on a flatboat at ten dollars per month) have been put down here as the candidate of pride, wealth, and aristocratic family distinction. Yet so, chiefly, it was. There was, too, the strangest combination of church influence against me. Baker is a Campbellite; and therefore, as I suppose, with few exceptions got all that church. My wife has some relations in the Presbyterian churches, and some with the Episcopal churches; and therefore, wherever it would tell, I was set down as either the one or the other, while it was everywhere contended that no Christian ought to go for me, because I belonged to no church, was suspected of being a deist, and had talked about fighting a duel. With all these things, Baker, of course, had nothing to do. Nor do I complain of them. As to his own church going for him, I think that was right enough, and as to the influences I have spoken of in the other, though they were very strong, it would be grossly untrue and unjust to charge that they acted upon them in a body or were very near so. I only mean that those influences levied a tax of a considerable per cent. upon my strength throughout the religious controversy. But enough of this.

You say that in choosing a candidate for Congress you have an equal right with Sangamon, and in this you are undoubtedly correct. In agreeing to withdraw if the Whigs of Sangamon should go against me, I did not mean that they alone were worth consulting, but that if she, with her heavy delegation, should be against me, it would be impossible for me to succeed, and therefore I had as well decline. And in relation to Menard having rights, permit me fully to recognize them, and to express the opinion that, if she and Mason act circumspectly, they will in the convention be able so far to enforce their rights as to decide absolutely which one of the candidates shall be successful. Let me show the reason of this. Hardin, or some other Morgan candidate, will get Putnam, Marshall, Woodford, Tazewell, and Logan—making sixteen. Then you and Mason, having three, can give the victory to either side.

You say you shall instruct your delegates for me, unless I object. I certainly shall not object. That would be too pleasant a compliment for me to tread in the dust. And besides, if anything should happen (which, however, is not probable) by which Baker should be thrown out of the fight, I would be at liberty to accept the nomination if I could get it. I do, however, feel myself bound not to hinder him in any way from getting the nomination. I should despise myself were I to attempt it. I think, then, it would be proper for your meeting to appoint three delegates and to instruct them to go for some one as the first choice, some one else as a second, and perhaps some one as a third; and if in those instructions I were named as the first choice, it would gratify me very much. If you wish to hold the balance of power, it is important for you to attend to and secure the vote of Mason also: You should be sure to have men appointed delegates that you know you can safely confide in. If yourself and James Short were appointed from your county, all would be safe; but whether Jim's woman affair a year ago might not be in the way of his appointment is a question. I don't know whether you know it, but I know him to be as honorable a man as there is in the world. You have my permission, and even request, to show this letter to Short; but to no one else, unless it be a very particular friend who you know will not speak of it.

Yours as ever, A. LINCOLN.

P. S Will you write me again?

TO MARTIN M. MORRIS.
April 14, 1843.
FRIEND MORRIS:

I have heard it intimated that Baker has been attempting to get you or Miles, or both of you, to violate the instructions of the meeting that appointed you, and to go for him. I have insisted, and still insist, that this cannot be true. Surely Baker would not do the like. As well might Hardin ask me to vote for him in the convention. Again, it is said there will be an attempt to get up instructions in your county requiring you to go for Baker. This is all wrong. Upon the same rule, Why might not I fly from the decision against me in Sangamon, and get up instructions to their delegates to go for me? There are at least twelve hundred Whigs in the county that took no part, and yet I would as soon put my head in the fire as to attempt it. Besides, if any one should get the nomination by such extraordinary means, all harmony in the district would inevitably be lost. Honest Whigs (and very nearly all of them are honest) would not quietly abide such enormities. I repeat, such an attempt on Baker's part cannot be true. Write me at Springfield how the matter is. Don't show or speak of this letter.

A. LINCOLN

TO GEN. J. J. HARDIN.
SPRINGFIELD, May 11, 1843.
FRIEND HARDIN:

Butler informs me that he received a letter from you, in which you expressed some doubt whether the Whigs of Sangamon will support you cordially. You may, at once, dismiss all fears on that subject. We have already resolved to make a particular effort to give you the very largest majority possible in our county. From this, no Whig of the county dissents. We have many objects for doing it. We make it a matter of honor and pride to do it; we do it because we love the Whig cause; we do it because we like you personally; and last, we wish to convince you that we do not bear that hatred to Morgan County that you people have so long seemed to imagine. You will see by the journals of this week that we propose, upon pain of losing a barbecue, to give you twice as great a majority in this county as you shall receive in your own. I got up the proposal.

Who of the five appointed is to write the district address? I did the labor of writing one address this year, and got thunder for my reward. Nothing new here.

Yours as ever, A. LINCOLN.

P. S.—I wish you would measure one of the largest of those swords we took to Alton and write me the length of it, from tip of the point to tip of the hilt, in feet and inches. I have a dispute about the length.

A. L.

Lincoln's Gettysburg Address, given November 19, 1863 on the battlefield near Gettysburg, Pennsylvania, USA

Four score and seven years ago, our fathers brought forth upon this continent a new nation: conceived in liberty, and dedicated to the proposition that all men are created equal.

Now we are engaged in a great civil war ... testing whether that nation, or any nation so conceived and so dedicated ... can long endure. We are met on a great battlefield of that war.

We have come to dedicate a portion of that field as a final resting place for those who here gave their lives that this nation might live. It is altogether fitting and proper that we should do this.

But, in a larger sense, we cannot dedicate ... we cannot consecrate ... we cannot hallow this ground. The brave men, living and dead, who struggled here have consecrated it, far above our poor power to add or detract. The world will little note, nor long remember, what we say here, but it can never forget what they did here.

It is for us the living, rather, to be dedicated here to the unfinished work which they who fought here have thus far so nobly advanced. It is rather for us to be here dedicated to the great task remaining before us ... that from these honored dead we take increased devotion to that cause for which they gave the last full measure of devotion ... that we here highly resolve that these dead shall not have died in vain ... that this nation, under God, shall have a new birth of freedom ... and that government of the people ... by the people ... for the people ... shall not perish from this earth.

THE EMANCIPATION PROCLAMATION:

By the President of the United States of America:

A PROCLAMATION

Whereas on the 22nd day of September, A.D. 1862, a proclamation was issued by the President of the United States, containing, among other things, the following, to wit:

"That on the 1st day of January, A.D. 1863, all persons held as slaves within any State or designated part of a State the people whereof shall then be in rebellion against the United States shall be then, thenceforward, and forever free; and the executive government of the United States, including the military and naval authority thereof, will recognize and maintain the freedom of such persons and will do no act or acts to repress such persons, or any of them, in any efforts they may make for their actual freedom.

"That the executive will on the 1st day of January aforesaid, by proclamation, designate the States and parts of States, if any, in which the people thereof, respectively, shall then be in rebellion against the United States; and the fact that any State or the people thereof shall on that day be in good faith represented in the Congress of the United States by members chosen thereto at elections wherein a majority of the qualified voters of such States shall have participated shall, in the absence of strong countervailing testimony, be deemed conclusive evidence that such State and the people thereof are not then in rebellion against the United States."

Now, therefore, I, Abraham Lincoln, President of the United States, by virtue of the power in me vested as Commander-In-Chief of the Army and Navy of the United States in time of actual armed rebellion against the authority and government of the United States, and as a fit and necessary war measure for supressing said rebellion, do, on this 1st day of January, A.D. 1863, and in accordance with my purpose so to do, publicly proclaimed for the full period of one hundred days from the first day above mentioned, order and designate as the States and parts of States wherein the people thereof, respectively, are this day in rebellion against the United States the following, to wit:

Arkansas, Texas, Louisiana (except the parishes of St. Bernard, Palquemines, Jefferson, St. John, St. Charles, St. James, Ascension, Assumption, Terrebone, Lafourche, St. Mary, St. Martin, and Orleans, including the city of New Orleans), Mississippi, Alabama, Florida, Georgia, South Carolina, North Carolina, and Virginia (except the forty-eight counties designated as West Virginia, and also the counties of Berkeley, Accomac, Morthhampton, Elizabeth City, York, Princess Anne, and Norfolk, including the cities of Norfolk and Portsmouth), and which excepted parts are for the present left precisely as if this proclamation were not issued.

And by virtue of the power and for the purpose aforesaid, I do order and declare that all persons held as slaves within said designated States and parts of States are, and henceforward shall be, free; and that the Executive Government of the United States, including the military and naval authorities thereof, will recognize and maintain the freedom of said persons.

And I hereby enjoin upon the people so declared to be free to abstain from all violence, unless in necessary self-defence; and I recommend to them that, in all case when allowed, they labor faithfully for reasonable wages.

And I further declare and make known that such persons of suitable condition will be received into the armed service of the United States to garrison forts, positions, stations, and other places, and to man vessels of all sorts in said service.

And upon this act, sincerely believed to be an act of justice, warranted by the Constitution upon military necessity, I invoke the considerate judgment of mankind and the gracious favor of Almighty God.

www.ingramcontent.com/pod-product-compliance
Lightning Source LLC
Chambersburg PA
CBHW071434090426
42737CB00011B/1655